Does God Really Love Me?

TURNING GOD'S LOVE LOOSE IN YOUR LIFE

Earl D. Wilson

INTERVARSITY PRESS
DOWNERS GROVE, ILLINOIS 60515

InterVarsity Press is the book-publishing division of Inter-Varsity Christian Fellowship, a student movement active on campus at hundreds of universities, colleges and schools of nursing. For information about local and regional activities, write IVCF, 233 Langdon St., Madison, WI 53703.

Distributed in Canada through InterVarsity Press, 860 Denison St., Unit 3, Markham, Ontario L3R 4H1, Canada.

All Scripture quotations, unless otherwise stated, are from The Holy Bible: New International Version. Copyright © 1978 by the New York Bible Society. Used by permission of Zondervan Bible Publishers.

Cover photograph: Carlos Vergara

ISBN 0-87784-514-X

Printed in the United States of America

Library of Congress Cataloging in Publication Data
Wilson, Earl D., 1939-
    Does God really love me?

    Includes bibliographies.
    1. God—Love.   2. Love (theology).   I. Title.
BT140.W57   1986   231'.6   86-10616
ISBN 0-87784-514-X (pbk.)

16	15	14	13	12	11	10	9	8	7	6	5	4	3	2	1
99	98	97	96	95	94	93	92	91	90	89	88	87	86		

This book is affectionately dedicated to four special pastors and their wives who have taught me through word and deed about God's great love. Thanks to Dallas and Dorothy Keck, Wesley and Vivian Hustad, Tom and Lois Kramer, and Robert and Shirley Westgate. There have been others, but the impact of these eight people has been extra special.

1
WHY ALL THIS TALK ABOUT LOVE?

*D*onna *was a sophomore who majored in having a good* time. But one evening she went to a meeting sponsored by a campus Christian group. Jack was the speaker. Donna was amazed. Here was the first person she had ever met who could talk about love and who also seemed to be a loving person. "My parents always wanted something in return for their love," Donna said, "and so do most of my friends. After hearing Jack, the concept of unconditional love became a possibility for me."

But Donna put the experience in the back of her mind and once more became immersed in campus life. She tried to escape the hound of heaven, but unsuccessfully. Finally, in despair, she let her Christian friend Mary take her to talk more with Jack. Eventually Donna became a Christian, and her friendship with Jack and his wife,

Sharon, began to grow. The more she was around them, the more she was amazed by their love. Nonetheless, Donna could not forsake the good times. Her free use of alcohol and sex put her in a terrible tension. On the one hand, she knew that Jack and Sharon were different. Their lifestyle confirmed the truth they talked about. She wanted to share that peace and closeness. On the other hand, she enjoyed the good feelings, the comfort, the closeness she felt in her own lifestyle. Finally she agreed to see me for counseling to please Jack even though she had told him she was giving up Christianity.

After we got to know each other, I began to ask Donna about her view of God. She believed that God loved her enough to die for her, but she couldn't believe that he could love her enough to be her friend. Her thinking was immobolized. Donna's intellectual understanding of a relationship with God was theological and cold. Since she couldn't accept the fact that God would want to be close to her, she decided to go against his will to find closeness and acceptance in other ways. She was caught in a deadly trap which she had created. "If I could just understand love the way Jack and Sharon do," she cried, "then maybe I could have a chance."

Living in the Sun
In the twenty years that I have counseled, I have found that literally thousands of people suffer from the same dilemma as Donna. They want to feel loved. They believe in a loving God, but they don't know how to get close to him. Nick said, "The more confused I become about God's love, the more unlovable I feel. I guess I don't trust him to make me happy. I keep taking things into my own hands. I've just made a big mess of my life."

All this confusion about the love of God is not too difficult to understand when we consider that both love and God are beyond our human comprehension. The Bible makes definitive statements about who God is and the way he loves us, but these statements cannot be understood apart from faith. Fully appreciating God's love can never be an intellectual exercise alone. It has to involve our whole person.

You can sit in Chicago on a cold winter morning and watch a weather report which tells you that it is eighty-four degrees and sunny in Los Angeles. But it does you little good to know that there are others who are not experiencing your wind chill of twenty below. You see a video of spectators in tank tops and shorts basking in the beautiful sun, and how you wish you were there! Those Californians seem to know what sunshine is all about. They can tell you both intellectually and emotionally that it is eighty-four degrees. It seems to permeate their whole lives.

Jack and Sharon are like sunbathers. They allow the warmth of God's love to touch them. They go where the sun is and take the time to enjoy it. Donna wanted the warmth too. But rather than go where it is, she tried to manufacture it herself. She hoped that her love affairs would help her forget the cold, but it just didn't work that way. She was left with the legacy of loneliness, guilt and disobedience to God. Perhaps she was afraid to trust God and his love. Perhaps she, like many others, had never really understood it.

John the apostle makes an astounding statement: "We know and rely on the love God has for us. God is love. Whoever lives in love lives in God, and God in him" (1 Jn 4:16). There is a connection between believing in

God, living in his love and learning to be more loving yourselves. Love starts with God because it is his nature. Love isn't natural for us. But we can share in it by sharing in God's nature. It's like choosing to live in the tropics rather than the arctic.

Consider how love is portrayed on a sampling of current television shows. Now contrast that with how love is presented in the following Scripture passage: "Love is patient, love is kind. It does not envy, it does not boast, it is not proud. It is not rude, it is not self-seeking, it is not easily angered, it keeps no record of wrongs. Love does not delight in evil but rejoices with the truth. It always protects, always trusts, always hopes, always perseveres. Love never fails" (1 Cor 13:4-8).

There is a lot of talk about love today because all of us want it so desperately. But because our understanding of the source of love is so superficial, the talk is usually empty and not followed by action.

In his book *Forty Ways to Say I Love You,* Bjorge states, "Love is dynamic, growing, constantly creating new songs of spirit and substance."[1] People who feel unloved and isolated from God are unlikely to conjure up this dynamic, creative, growing condition. Indeed the Bible says, "We love, because he first loved us," and "Dear friends, since God so loved us, we also ought to love one another" (1 Jn 4:19, 11).

The progression seems obvious. First, we accept God's great gift of love in giving Jesus Christ to die for us. ("For God so loved the world that he gave his one and only Son, that whoever believes in him shall not perish but have eternal life"—Jn 3:16.) After this step of regeneration or rebirth, we begin to experience God's love emotionally as well as intellectually. (We start living in the sun.) Third, as we learn to live in God's love, we are able to pass on the love of God to others. In fact, it is God's desire that we embody his love. Our arms become his arms. He wants us to wrap them around other people who need to understand his great love. But since most Christians feel unloved by God and by others, they don't risk reaching out with God's love. But as we come to understand the nature of God's love more fully, we will be energized to create new ways of loving which can bring even more satisfaction to our lives than the selfish substitutes for love portrayed in much contemporary literature and drama.

In Search of the Sun

All of us are compelled by an inner drive to find love. But we respond to this urge in many different ways. Some search for it in soap operas, some in busy relationships, some in success and achievement. And some give up the search altogether and callous themselves to the world and to feelings.

Tom had tried everything. As a young child he wanted so much to please his parents. He grew up with the idea that if he could just do better, then he would feel loved. The harder he tried the more elusive his parents' love seemed to be. By the time Tom entered high school he was tired of trying to earn love. He was tired of being so close and yet so far away.

It didn't take long for him to discover a group of students who felt exactly as he did. They were fringe people, wanting to get on the inside but never quite able to find the key. Tom sensed an acceptance with his new friends. He wouldn't go so far as to say that they loved him, but at least they understood and didn't put a lot of pressure on him. The less pressure Tom felt, the more he began to drift. Slowly his studies became more and more pointless. He began to search for love in capsules, bottles and needles. Whatever love his friends had for him was now obscured by the deadening effect of the drugs. "I don't feel loved," Tom said, "but at least I don't feel anything."

After he nearly died from an accidental overdose, Tom went from drugs to meditation. Maybe love was within himself. He knew he couldn't go on the way he was. This helped for a while. His system became free of foreign substances, and his brain began to be useful to him again. There was even a hint of self-respect. He was back at a place where he could once again give to people. If he was ever going to feel loved, it was now. He wanted to give love and he wanted to receive it. The only problem was he didn't know how.

Tom had what I call impacted feelings. He possessed an emotion (in this case love), but the means of expressing or receiving it were restrained by other feelings such as fear or anger. Tom discovered that he didn't trust the expressions of love sent to him and that he was afraid to express love himself for fear that he wouldn't seem genuine. Love was there, but it was imprisoned, held in check.

Love, like other emotions, is essential to life. Yet it is so imperfectly expressed in our human interactions. 'Our emotions are a gift from God for we were created as emotional beings. Because of the fall, man's emotional life often becomes distorted. But our emotions as such should never be despised, expelled, ignored, or even neglected."[2]

Can we find love apart from God? The answer is no

and yes. In the truest sense of the word there is no love apart from God because (as we will discuss more fully in chapter five) God is the only source of love. Our answer, however, must be qualified. There are many people in the world who do not know God but who still love. It is the residual effect of being created by God. They can't help themselves.

Tom felt this love from his new friends. He also experienced the effects of love since in his meditation he was not too far removed from the source. But Tom was doing more talking about love than he was giving, and he was hearing more talk about love than he was receiving. Why? Because God was only faintly in the picture. Talk of love stimulates need and it may hold the line on human desperation, but the status quo is just not satisfactory. We need a revolution in love, a revolution that will turn the source of love loose on us and through us to other people. Such a revolution will give full meaning to the words of Jesus Christ: "A new commandment I give you: Love one another. As I have loved you, so you must love one another. All men will know that you are my disciples if you love one another" (Jn 13:34-35).

The purpose of this book is to take you on a new adventure, the adventure of learning to love God. We will seek to discover how God's love differs from our current misconceptions. Indeed, I want to share my views of just how personal and extravagant God's love really is. I want to teach you how to savor that love much the same way the sunbather savors the sun.

2
GOD'S EXTRAVAGANT LOVE

*D*o you know someone who is extravagant? I'm talking about the kind of person who buys you dinner and then insists that you eat the most expensive desert. And at Christmas time he just can't be outdone. He buys you two presents instead of one. His kindness and hospitality seem to have no limits. He's always on the lookout for a way to do something good for you.

My daughter Marcie treats her younger sisters that way. She knows that they enjoy collecting stickers. So she can hardly keep herself from buying them stickers every day. She loves to see the smile on their faces and the excitement they show when they receive her gifts. Marcie gives and gives because it is her nature to do so. She just keeps pouring it on.

The Bible says that's the way God loves us. "How

great is the love the Father has lavished on us, that we should be called children of God! And that is what we are!" (1 Jn 3:1).

The Father hasn't just shown his love to us. He hasn't just told us about it. He has covered us with it. One year I watched a ticker-tape parade after the Pittsburg Steelers won the Super Bowl. The coach and the players were covered with confetti, a symbol of their fans' love and admiration. Streamer after streamer came down from the tall buildings. The players were so touched that many had tears in their eyes. Can you imagine any of them trying to stay calm and unexcited? They were being loved and they embraced it fully. No one stopped to have an intellectual discussion of the social-psychological dynamics of large crowds. They just enjoyed what was happening. And they did exactly the right thing. The only way to enjoy extravagance is to sit back and soak it up. Notice how Jesus reacted when he received extravagant love.

While he was in Bethany, reclining at the table in the home of a man known as Simon the Leper, a woman came with an alabaster jar of very expensive perfume, made of pure nard. She broke the jar and poured the perfume on his head.

Some of those present were saying indignantly to one another, "Why this waste of perfume? It could have been sold for more than a year's wages and the money given to the poor." And they rebuked her harshly.

"Leave her alone," said Jesus. "Why are you bothering her? *She has done a beautiful thing to me.* The poor you will always have with you, and you can help them any time you want. But you will not always have me.

She did what she could. She poured perfume on my body beforehand to prepare for my burial. I tell you the truth, wherever the gospel is preached throughout the world, what she has done will also be told, in memory of her." (Mk 14:3-9)

Let me emphasize the key phrase, "She has done a beautiful thing to me." Jesus noticed. He got involved. He allowed himself to experience the full significance of what was happening. Some of the others became legalistic and critical, but he just accepted the expression of love in the way it was given.

We need to look for the ways God is lavishing his love on us and then take the time to enjoy that love. We know that his love in sending Christ to die for us was extravagant. It is difficult to understand that the Son of God would die for me even if I were perfect. It's even more incredible that he would die for me with all my faults. As Paul wrote, "Very rarely will anyone die for a righteous man, though for a good man someone might possibly dare to die. But God demonstrates his own love for us in this: While we were still sinners, Christ died for us" (Rom 5:7-8). In other words, he gave his best for me even at my worst.

For too many Christians their awareness of God's extravagance stops here. Not that God's extravagant love stops. Their awareness stops. If your eyes and ears are open, you will see that he just keeps pouring it on.

King David allowed himself to see the full measure of God's love.

I praise you because I am fearfully
   and wonderfully made;
your works are wonderful,
I know that full well.

Beyond the Expected

Many people *believe* that God's love is great and wonderful, that he lavished this love on them. But their belief is academic. It doesn't apply to them personally.

What are some of the ways in which God shows his extravagant love? Let's start with life and breath. God doesn't owe us anything. He chooses to keep us alive because he loves us. We are told not to worry. God's extravagant love will take care of us. "Therefore I tell you, do not worry about your life, what you will eat or drink; or about your body, what you will wear. Is not life more important than food, and the body more important than clothes? Look at the birds of the air; they do not sow or reap or store away in barns, and yet your heavenly Father feeds them. Are you not much more valuable than they?" (Mt 6:25-26).

I see God's extravagant love when he is patient with me. I flounder and disobey, but he doesn't throw me out. He asks me to come back. God knows how to treat people. As my pastor says, his love for us *is* outstanding. He is merciful. He doesn't get angry quickly.

As Paul expressed it, "I was shown mercy so that in me, the worst of sinners, Christ Jesus might display his unlimited patience as an example for those who would believe on him and receive eternal life" (1 Tim 1:16).

Paul was so excited about God's mercy and unlimited patience that he couldn't stop without sounding praise and adoration to God. If we don't take time to acknowledge the ways God's love is extravagant, we will gripe instead of worship. Even when the Israelites under Moses were receiving bread and quail from heaven, they complained rather than notice how extravagant God's love had been to feed them so often and so well (Ex 16).

God's extravagance is often shown to us through people who go beyond what is expected. When Sandy, my wife, was going through some difficult times, she called our friend Linda in Nebraska. Linda listened, prayed, counseled and confronted. She did everything one could ask. About a half-hour after the two hung up, the telephone rang.

It was Linda.

"I've decided to fly out to be with you."

"But, Linda, you can't fly out all the way to Portland. You can't afford it. It is just too extravagant."

"I know, but God's love is extravagant and he wants me to be with you. See you at the airport."

Sandy was overwhelmed and greatly appreciative. Linda came and God used her to help Sandy through the difficult time. We will never forget the lesson which Linda taught us. God's love is extravagant. He knows exactly what we need.

Sometimes God chooses to show his love through strangers. I took my son Mike to participate in a western regional wrestling tournament in Washington state. It was high level competition, and Mike was nervous. He felt alone and afraid. His dad is a great cheerleader, but not a wrestling coach. His first opponent was from Montana. Mike was his equal physically, but because of Mike's inexperience he was defeated. As I stood on the edge of the mat trying to help my young son who was choking back the tears of defeat, a hand touched my shoulder. It was a huge Montana cowboy with a large feathered hat.

"Is this your boy?" he asked. I nodded and he said, "Do you mind if I talk to him?"

"Not at all," I said and stepped aside.

For the next ten minutes this big cowboy gave my son a free coaching clinic. He not only instructed him, he also built him up and restored his confidence. I stood watching as the cowboy took off his big hat and got right down on the mat with Mike. Tears flooded my eyes as I saw the beauty of what was taking place.

Finally the cowboy coach said, "You got that?" Mike nodded with a big smile. One more thing the coach said, "You only get better when you lose. You are a good man. Don't forget that."

I stood there crying and praising God. "God," I said, "you are extravagant. You can even use a rough cowboy coach to show one of your young children how much he is loved."

Mike came over and said, "That was pretty neat."

"It sure was," I replied. "Let's go get something to drink before your old dad gets emotional."

These experiences have taught me to look for the ways God expresses his extravagant love. I've learned to appreciate the sunshine. I've learned to appreciate what the Bible says about God's great forgiveness. I've learned to appreciate the special love that is shown to me by my wife and my friends. I have even learned to appreciate the love that may come my way from strangers in cowboy hats.

The songwriter Annie Johnson Flint put it succinctly.

His love has no limit; His grace has no measure;
His pow'r has no boundary known unto men.
For out of His infinite riches in Jesus
He giveth and giveth and giveth again.[1]

Ask, Seek, Knock

Jesus often spoke of the extravagant love of the Father.

Ask and it will be given to you; seek and you will find; knock and the door will be opened to you. For everyone who asks receives; he who seeks finds; and to him who knocks, the door will be opened.

Which of you, if his son asks for bread, will give him a stone? Or if he asks for a fish, will give him a snake? If you, then, though you are evil, know how to give good gifts to your children, how much more will your Father in heaven give good gifts to those who ask him! In everything, do to others what you would have them do to you, for this sums up the Law and the Prophets. (Mt 7:7-12)

This passage from the Sermon on the Mount gives us some ideas on how to get in touch with God's extravagant love for us. First, action is needed. Do something—ask, seek, knock. Next, expect results—receiving, finding, opening. The pattern seems so simple. But God has promised us great things in following it.

If he is so willing to be extravagant, then why do I feel so poor or weak at times? James 4:2 gives the answer: "You do not have, because you do not ask God." God's extravagance is hindered most by our reluctance.

I remember seeing a child sitting on Santa's lap at Christmas time. He had a bag of toys and was just waiting to pass them out. He asked the child what she wanted but she didn't answer. "Ask me for a present," he continued. She sat there paralyzed, knowing Santa wanted to give her a toy but afraid to ask. If you want to see God's extravagance, all you have to do is open your mouth and ask. With God, the have-nots are the ask-nots.

Asking is not the only action God wants us to take. Jesus said, "Seek, and you will find." Pursue what you desire from God. Step out and go after it. God responds to our steps of faith by helping us to discover what we want or need. A parable Jesus told illustrates the point: "The kingdom of heaven is like treasure hidden in a field. When a man found it, he hid it again, and then in his joy went and sold all he had and bought that field" (Mt 13:44). The parable in the next two verses is similar. A merchant was seeking the highest quality pearls. Then he found one that was of such great value that he sold everything he had to buy it. That was an extraordinary pearl.

When we discover God's extravagance, we still have one more step to take. We need to buy. If we want to receive God's greatest blessings, we have to pay the price. We don't need to earn the blessing, but in order to possess it, action is essential. If you seek excellence, for example, you will have to pay the price of working to develop the excellent abilities God has lavished on you. When you seek, you will find. Trust the Father and give it all that you have to possess the beautiful pearl.

Asking. Seeking. The third action suggested for getting in touch with God's extravagant love is knocking. Knock, Jesus says, and the door will be opened.

I told Gary I would pick him up at his house and then we would drive to the weekend retreat together. We were both looking forward to a great time. The only problem was that I lost his address. I knew about where he lived, but I really didn't know exactly which door he was behind. So I knew I had to try some doors.

For a moment or two I felt like backing off and forgetting it. Knocking on doors is difficult, especially in an unfamiliar neighborhood. I knocked at several doors where there was no one home—or at least no one home who wanted to talk to me. There were others who said they were sorry but they couldn't help me because they didn't know Gary. Finally, I knocked and the door swung open. My friend said, "Hi, I've been anxious for you to get here. Come on in."

Just as I had to work to find my friend, there are times when I must go out of my way if I expect to receive God's blessing. Knocking on doors requires faith, but why worry? God loves to respond to our faith just as Gary was anxious to answer the door.

God is anxious to give us good things. In Matthew 7 Jesus says that a father, even an evil one, won't give his children stones if they ask for bread, or snakes if they ask for fish. So how much more will our Father in heaven, who is the essence of goodness, give us good things if we ask him?

Too many Christians act like scared puppies. We are hungry, but we are afraid to approach our master who has the food. We start to approach and then run away. What is it that God has in his hand? Is it a stick or is it a bone? Is it bread or a rock? You won't know until you take the risk of getting close. "Come near to God and he will come near to you" (Ja 4:8).

Love without a Hook

Have you ever tried to give away money on the street? It may surprise you but people are skeptical and reluctant to receive it. You know the old saying, "There is no such thing as a free lunch." Or as my dad used to say, "You just don't get something for nothing." We have trained ourselves to look beyond the gift to the underlying motivation of the giver. As one client said when her husband was nice to her, "There must be a hook. He wants something, or he's trying to cover up for something."

God's love is hard to understand because he doesn't need anything from us, and he doesn't have a thing to hide. His love is endless and his motives are entirely pure. But his love is difficult to appreciate when all the love we have experienced in life has been tainted. God doesn't need or want to manipulate us. He just wants to see us respond to his love.

The most powerful illustration of love without a hook is given by John in his first epistle. "This is how we know what love is: Jesus Christ laid down his life for us. And we ought to lay down our lives for our brothers" (1 Jn 3:16). It is difficult to believe that a man who died for me had no ulterior motive, that I don't have to watch for the hook, that I can just accept his love without giving anything in return.

If someone says to me, "You look nice today," I may say to myself, "I'll bet he thinks I look like a bum most of the time and is just trying to shape me up." Looking for the hook keeps me from accepting the expression of love.

Of course it is true that some people show love to us because they want us to love them in return. In some cases their need for love approaches the desperation level. In such situations we may feel that if we accept even the smallest expression of love, we will be doomed forever to give love back to them whether we feel like it or not. God's love is not like that. God wants us to love him voluntarily, not because he traps us. God is powerful enough to demand our love, but he chooses instead to ask for our love and wait patiently for our response. He doesn't bribe. He doesn't bully. He invites.

And when he invites you to dinner, you aren't expected to come with a hot dish in hand to contribute. He provides the full meal. With his love there is no hook.

Three Love Gifts

I began this chapter by comparing God's extravagant love with people who delight in giving gifts. What kind of a gift-giver is God? Let's look at the three basic kinds of gifts he gives.

The first is what we might expect most. When we think of the word *gift*, we usually associate it with the word *present*—like a birthday present or a Christmas present. Luke had a specific gift in mind: "If you then, though you are evil, know how to give good gifts to your children, how much more will your Father in heaven give the Holy Spirit to those who ask him!" (Lk 11:13). Likewise, John speaks of God's gift of the Holy Spirit as a present—a present which comforts (Jn 14:16). He consoles us in our grief and sorrow. He encourages us when we are low. He is our loyal companion, a true friend. He gives the gift of comfort.

The second kind of gift, the kind most commonly used in the New Testament, is connected with the spiritual gifts. This type of gift is given for the purpose of enabling or equipping us to build up Christ's body. God prepares us to serve him or to serve other Christians. In 1 Corinthians 12 Paul gives us a list of many such gifts:

> Now to each one the manifestation of the Spirit is given for the common good. To one there is given through the Spirit the message of wisdom, to another the message of knowledge by means of the same Spirit, to another faith by the same Spirit, to another gifts of healing by that one Spirit, to another miraculous powers, to another prophecy, to another the ability to

distinguish between spirits, to another the ability to speak in different kinds of tongues, and to still another the interpretation of tongues. All these are the work of one and the same Spirit, and he gives them to each man, just as he determines. (1 Cor 12:7-11)

The list is not exhaustive. God's love is more extravagant than that. But it does point out some of the marvelous things he does for us.

Unfortunately, the idea of spiritual gifts has often been distorted. We tend to emphasize what we see as the most sensational—healing or prophecy—without realizing that every gift is of equal value to God and his people. We also tend to believe that only the most spiritual people are given gifts. Such a view tends to create a kind of Christian caste system in which many people flaunt what they have received. But "the body is not made up of one part but of many" (1 Cor 12:14). We all belong to each other. We all have a contribution to make to the body of Christ in the form of the spiritual gifts God has given. God's love is extravagant enough to include everyone.

As remarkable as spiritual gifts are, the third type of gift God gives is even more amazing. The word translated "gift" comes from the Greek word *doron,* which carries the idea of a sacrifice or an offering. It is used in the phrase "if you are offering your gift at the altar" in Matthew 5:23. In Hebrews 5:1 the same word is used to refer to the high priestly duties of offering sacrifices and gifts for sins. But this last type of gift is even more unusual because God is both the giver and the sacrifice. This gift is called by many different names: the gift of God, the gift of grace, the gift of the Holy Spirit, the gift of righteousness. It cannot be stated more clearly than in these well-known words, "For God so loved the world that he gave his one and only Son, that whoever believes in him shall not perish but have eternal life" (Jn 3:16).

God sacrificed himself for you and me. But he doesn't even stop there. After giving himself *for* us, he then gives himself *to* us. He chooses to live within us. He gives us his very nature. We become new creatures. Before we received the gift we were without hope. After the sacrifice we are one with God himself. Is it any wonder that Paul wrote, "Thanks be to God for his indescribable gift" (2 Cor 9:15)?

Understanding this gift helps us understand some of the difficult passages of Scripture. Notice the use of *doron* in the following verse: "It is impossible for those who have once been enlightened, who have tasted the heavenly *gift*, who have shared in the Holy Spirit, who have tasted the goodness of the word of God and the powers of the coming age, if they fall away, to be brought back to repentance, because to their loss they are crucifying the Son of God all over again and subjecting him to public disgrace" (Heb 6:4-6).

The heavenly gift is so great that if it were to be lost it could never be restored because it would require that Christ die again. I believe the idea of losing the gift is hypothetical. The writer mentions it to underscore just how great the gift actually is. If you could lose the gift, the loss would be irreplaceable because it would require a totally new sacrifice of Christ. But Paul used the same Greek word for gift when he wrote, "For God's gifts and his call are irrevocable" (Rom 11:29).

Soaking Up God's Extravagance
I was standing in a clearing in the Colorado mountains

watching the sun come up and wishing I had a better illustration of the way God lavishes his extravagant love on us. I was waiting for breakfast when the call of the cook startled me back to reality. "We can begin to eat now," she said as she turned the bacon and put another hot cake on the griddle.

I fixed my attention on the bull's eye (a hot cake with an egg cooked in the center) I had ordered. I patiently waited for the syrup as I watched the young boy next to me flood his plate with the stuff. Then it hit me! That was it! I had my illustration. My young friend hadn't just put syrup on his hot cakes. He had lavished it on them. I took the large container and quickly accomplished the same thing.

Half-embarrassed I said, "It's hard not to put too much on, isn't it?"

He nodded and then said, "But look at my plate." Most of the excess had been absorbed. The hot cake was literally permeated with the sweet maple flavor. The lad smiled with delight and took his first big bite. "Hmm, good," he said. I winked at him and turned my attention to my own breakfast.

I mused as I breathed the crisp mountain air and savored my food. God loves us just like my young friend and I pour syrup. He fills our plates with his goodness. He also wants us to soak it up. To experience the blessing of God's love I have to be willing to let it permeate me. Hot cakes can do that. Stones can't. We need to be receptive to all the extravagant love God gives to us. He wants us to just soak it up.

3

SAVORING: THE SECRET TO FEELING LOVED

*O*ver the last ten years I have asked dozens of people to tell me the first time they really felt loved by God. The answers have been astonishing. More than half said they were not sure they ever felt loved by God—or anyone else for that matter.

Something is obviously wrong here. Scripture says that God is lavishing his great love on us, but the majority of the people I have asked do not feel loved at all. Is Scripture exaggerating or is there something else awry?

As I've asked people why they answered as they did, I've gotten a variety of responses. Vikki told me, "God must love me because he doesn't lie, but you sure couldn't prove that to my feelings."

Don said, "I don't spend much time thinking about

God's love. I guess I spend more time worrying about his vengeance."

Mark said, "I don't think about God at all. I guess I am afraid to."

We often view God in two different ways at the same time. With our minds we believe that we are accepted and loved, but with our hearts we do not feel that love.

How can we bridge this gap? How can we bring our minds and hearts together? I think the secret can be found in *savoring.*

We know what it means to taste food. Some meals are just delightful. They smell good, they taste good, and we relish the experience of eating them. This is savoring.

The Case of the Missing Blackberries
Wild blackberries are a luxury to me. When I see roadsides and yards covered with heavily loaded bushes, I can hardly wait to do battle with the brush and thorns until I have eaten my fill.

Unexpectedly an opportunity of a lifetime came my way when our family was visiting friends. Our hostess, Eunice, made me an offer I couldn't refuse. She said that if I would watch all the children (nine of them between our two families) while she and Sandy went shopping, she would let me eat all the blackberries I wanted. She further tempted me by showing me a three-pound coffee can which her son, Scott, had filled to the brim that very morning with Clackamas County's finest. I played it cool and acted as though I could take it or leave it. But inside my excitement began to rise.

The car had barely begun to back out of the driveway when I found the berries and a lawn chair on the deck and began to gorge myself. "The children can take care of themselves," I said to myself. "I'm going to take care of these berries." I joyfully began stuffing them into my mouth with both hands, pausing only long enough to wipe the succulent juice from my beard.

I had eaten at least a pound when a thought suddenly lodged itself in my mind. "I wonder what these taste like?" I was shocked by the question. How could I have eaten that many berries without really appreciating how they tasted? "I sure hope no one was watching me," I thought in embarrassment.

Then and there I decided to savor those berries. "I want to enjoy every aspect of them." With this new plan I turned my attention back to my can of fruit. But this time I chose to eat them one at a time. I allowed myself to inhale the sweet smell. My tastebuds lingered over the wonderfully sweet but tangy flavor. I even held the berries between my tongue and the roof of my mouth to enjoy their texture better. The experience was fabulous. I enjoyed it so much I spent the rest of the afternoon polishing off my prize.

When Eunice and Sandy returned, they both just looked at me and at the empty container. "I hope you didn't make yourself sick," Sandy said.

Eunice laughed and said, "It looks like you had a good time." It was amazing but even the children had survived the afternoon.

To savor is to take the time to enjoy. When a person savors food, we call him or her a connoisseur. When people savor an athletic team, we call them fans. When we savor God, we call it worship. The Bible puts it this way, "Where your treasure is, there your heart will be also" (Mt 6:21). When we treasure something, we take the time to look at it and to hold it. We spend time rehearsing its positive qualities.

Savoring is an active process. It involves our whole being—especially the emotions. Notice the words used by King Solomon as he savored his spouse.

How beautiful you are, my darling!
Oh how beautiful!
Your eyes behind your veil are doves.
Your hair is like a flock of goats
    descending from Mount Gilead.
Your teeth are like a flock of sheep just shorn,
    coming up from the washng.
Each has its twin;
    not one of them is alone.
Your lips are like a scarlet ribbon;
    your mouth is lovely.
Your temples behind your veil
    are like the halves of a pomegranate.
Your neck is like the tower of David,
    built with elegance;
on it hang a thousand shields,
    all of them shields of warriors.
Your two breasts are like two fawns,
    like twin fawns of a gazelle
    that browse among the lilies. (Song 4:1-5)

Solomon focused on every aspect of the beauty of his spouse. He wasn't going to be robbed of even one fine detail. He treasured her and that was where his heart was. This is savoring.

Slow Down and Remember

The first step in learning to savor God's love is to slow down enough to be able to recognize the ways in which God has loved you. Just as I had to take time to look at and taste the individual blackberries, we need to pause to identify the special ways God is loving us.

Before Ned became a Christian, he had prayed that God would show him how he loved him. Later Ned prayed another prayer. He asked God to help him through a tough time with his parents. God answered that prayer, and Ned took the time to acknowledge the way God had lovingly revealed himself.

Later Ned told me, "I don't know whether it was a miracle or not, but my problem is solved and all my objections to becoming a Christian have been wiped away one by one."

I reminded Ned that God loved him too much to let him escape. He grinned at me and said, "I'm not sure I want to escape anymore." When Ned had slowed down to look for God's love, he found it.

Once you have recognized the ways in which God has loved you and is loving you, the next step is to rehearse. By this I mean reminding ourselves of the ways we have experienced God's love. If we don't, we'll forget them and some of our old fears will return. On the other hand, the more we rehearse God's love, the more we enjoy it day after day.

Satan tries to take away our pleasant memories of the many ways God has loved us. So if we stop remembering the goodness of God, we become vulnerable to bitterness or disappointment. The more we remember with confidence what God has done for us in the beginning, the more we will truly be partakers of Christ. Savoring the ways God showed his love to us yesterday will help us to feel loved today. Emotions are built on memories. The more we choose to remember being loved by God, the more we will feel loved today.

Peanut Butter and Honey

In addition to slowing down and remembering, savoring is looking for new expressions of God's love. Some years ago I traveled to Iran by myself for three weeks of speaking engagements. I knew I would be lonely, and my wife knew I would be lonely. I wasn't sure why she had volunteered to pack my clothes, but when I arrived in Tehran I found a love note. She wanted to express her love in deed and word. I enjoyed the note. I read it over and over again as tears of joy filled my eyes. Eventually I put it in a safe place and continued unpacking.

To my surprise and delight, there was another note. I enjoyed it too, taking time to cherish it. But now I looked for another. Soon I found it. Indeed, there seemed to be no end. The notes of love were in socks, in pockets, between shirts. All I had to do was recognize them and let them touch my lonely being. Even when I finally exhausted the supply of notes, the love was still there. I was free to go back the next day and enjoy them all over again.

We can savor God's love by reading the Bible in much the same way I read Sandy's love notes. We can go back to read and experience God's love day after day. David wrote,

Let the morning bring me word of your unfailing
love,
for I have put my trust in you.
Show me the way I should go,
for to you I lift up my soul. (Ps 143:8)

This verse challenges us to look for God's lovingkindness each morning and offers an example of what savoring God actually is. We all need to lift up our souls to God.

Most New Testament letters begin with a greeting.

These openings usually contain some information about God or God's love which can be savored. Notice the greeting in Peter's second letter.

> Grace and peace be yours in abundance through the knowledge of God and of Jesus our Lord.
>
> His divine power has given us everything we need for life and godliness through our knowledge of him who called us by his own glory and goodness. Through these he has given us his very great and precious promises, so that through them you may participate in the divine nature and escape the corruption in the world caused by evil desires.
>
> For this very reason, make every effort to add to your faith goodness; and to goodness, knowledge. (2 Pet 1:2-5)

The "exceedingly great and precious promises" Peter wrote of are for us to savor. Through them we become like God. The more we savor the more we become like him. We become "partakers of the divine nature." If I savor too many blackberries I may become ill, but the more I savor God, the more I become like him.

In the introduction to his book *Growing Strong in the Seasons of Life* Charles Swindoll writes:

> The master is neither mute nor careless as He alters our times and changes our seasons. How wrong to trudge blindly and routinely through a lifetime of changing seasons without discovering answers to the new mysteries and learning to sing the new melodies! Seasons are designed to deepen us, to instruct us in the wisdom and ways of our God. To help us grow strong . . . like a tree planted by the rivers of water.[1]

In essence we have learned to savor God when we look for new expressions of God's love in each new season.

Savoring is discovering new answers and singing new melodies.

One final step in knowing how to savor God's love is to act on the expressions of love we have experienced. God's love was never meant to be hoarded so that it becomes stagnant. We are not to be cisterns. We are to be springs. I appreciate God's love the most when I act as a channel through which his great love is passed on to others. As John wrote, "Let us love one another, for love comes from God. Everyone who loves has been born of God and knows God. Whoever does not love does not know God, because God is love" (1 Jn 4:7-8).

The more we love, the more we know of God. The more we know of God and his extravagant love, the more we want to love others. Many people who don't feel loved by God think God's love is something to be received and stored rather than channeled to others. When people begin to give away God's love, they also begin to experience it.

Have you ever tried to make peanut butter and honey sandwiches without experiencing peanut butter and honey? It's impossible. Sooner or later in self-defense you have to taste what is running off your fingers. Even if you don't know much about peanut butter or honey, you will become excited as you see and discover what it can do for those you serve it to. "Taste and see that the LORD is good; blessed is the man who takes refuge in him" (Ps 34:8). And like peanut butter and honey, not only is God's love nutritious, it sticks with you.

The Difference Savoring Makes

When I talk about savoring I know I will be asked, "Does it really make a difference?" Sadly the world is full of skeptics. We don't really believe anything can change us.

By his own admission, Norm is a negative person. He has always tried to prove his own value by being negative about the value in other people. Eventually he recognized that he should be more positive and decided to try to work at it. The place to begin, he concluded, was to put more positive thoughts into his mind. Since the best source of positive thoughts that he could think of was the Bible, he began a habit of reading the Bible each morning just to look for positives.

It wasn't long before Norm began to feel less angry. "God just feels closer," Norm told me, "and I am not as bitter as I used to be." In a month or so his wife, Laura, began to notice a difference. He was more positive and less defensive about himself. He felt more loved by God and he became more proficient at expressing God's love to his wife. In essence he was choosing to savor God's love as expressed in Scripture. Laura would be the first to tell you that savoring really does make a difference.

I enjoy writing verse. Though the following may not be a masterpiece, it may help summarize the importance of savoring.

There once was a man who couldn't stay happy.
He tried to be nice but just ended up snappy.
He flooded his mind with jealousy and hate.
It tore down his life and affected his mate.

One day he decided his thinking must change.
"My mind," he thought, "I must rearrange."
He focused on Scripture and love and good will
And now he's so different his life is a thrill!

On the children's television show "Sesame Street," Oscar the Grouch lives in a garbage can. He loves to collect trash and enjoys only what is ugly, broken or sad. We laugh at Oscar. But I've met dozens of people who are just like him. Remarkably they spend most of their time dwelling on the negative. They have never learned how to savor the good—be it a sunset or God himself. Choosing to live with your head in a garbage can is a terrible but all too common choice.

It takes concerted effort to change negative thought patterns. But as with Norm, it is possible. I suggest people start with what is most tangible. What can I appreciate that is within three feet of me? I see my wife's picture, my telephone, my Bible, my coffee cup, my dolphin collection and a poster my daughter gave to me. These are things I value. I just took a few minutes to enjoy them and to say thanks to God for each one. I can't savor until I have stopped to notice what I value.

After we have practiced savoring things, we can turn our attention to people. What contribution is made to my life by each person I meet? My wife gives me joy. My children are fun and challenging. The gas station attendant is friendly and makes me feel welcome. My secretary is helpful and pleasant to work with. My day is a parade of people. Each person has some positive qualities which I can enjoy. But I must choose to focus on them.

Our appreciation of God is complete when we experience his love emotionally. I am not satisfied just to know that my wife loves me. I want to experience the emotions of feeling loved. I want to joyfully anticipate seeing her and talking with her. I want my love for her and her love for me to be complete.

When I first enrolled at Multnomah School of the Bi-

ble, my appreciation of God's love for me was pretty intellectual. I had all the right answers but not many feelings. I soon became involved with a new church. I don't
remember many things about the four years I fellow-
shiped with those people, but I do remember when we
got together to sing. Victor and Frieda Kundert taught
us a song which impressed me greatly.

I know God loves me,
And He will save me,
I know God loves me,
For He is love.

He sent me Jesus
The Loving Savior,
He sent me Jesus
Who set me free.

And this my song shall be:
I know God loves me,
I know God loves me,
For he is love.[2]

The more I sang that song and the more I spent time
with that group of people, the more I felt God's love.
Singing the melody over and over again helped me to
savor our great God. I even got to a place where I
couldn't stop singing it. As I would drive down the road
I would see Frieda at the piano with Victor's hand on her
shoulder. I would see their broad smiles as they led us
in the chorus, "I know God loves me for he is love."

Last Sunday when I walked into church, the preservice
worship had already begun. Dieter Zander was at the

piano with the microphone in front of him. He went from one chorus of worship to another. By the time I reached my seat I too was singing in full volume. "In moments like these we sing out a love song. We sing out a love song to Jesus."

After savoring God and his great love in this way, it was so natural for me to pray. "God, you do know how to love your children. Thanks for teaching me to savor because now I really do feel loved."

4

A SINNER LOOKS AT LOVE

We have all been trained to believe that God's love is conditional. We believe that he loves us just when we are good. And in addition to withholding his love when we are bad, he chooses to punish us as well. Our fear of God is real. When we sin we often distance ourselves from him just as Adam and Eve did in the garden. "Then the man and his wife heard the sound of the LORD God as he was walking in the garden in the cool of the day, and they hid from the LORD God among the trees of the garden. But the LORD God called to the man, 'Where are you?' " (Gen 3:8-9).

This kind of reaction highlights a number of reasonable questions. What happens to God's love for us when we sin? Does his anger over our sin supersede his desire to show his love to us? Does the fact that God cannot look upon sin mean that he can no longer shower his great love on us? What about his everlasting love? Is it only everlasting until we sin?

The nation Israel seemed to constantly test God's love. Time and time again they disobeyed and time and time again their sin brought them to the brink of destruction. The nation was punished by God, but the punishment did not mean that the love of God hesitated for a minute. As Jeremiah put it, " 'The people who survive the sword will find favor in the desert; I will come to give rest to Israel.' The LORD appeared to us in the past, saying: 'I have loved you with an everlasting love; I have drawn you with loving-kindness. I will build you up again and you will be rebuilt, O Virgin Israel' " (Jer 31:2-4).

These verses emphasize three important things about God's relationship to his people. He loves us. He draws us. He builds us up again. When we sin, God virtually jumps at the chance to move us beyond our sin so that he can shower his love on us again. We seem to be the ones that stall, not him. Notice the excitement which follows the verses quoted above. "Again you will take up your tambourines and go out to dance with the joyful. Again you will plant vineyards on the hills of Samaria; the farmers will plant them and enjoy their fruit" (Jer 31:4-5).

David: Sinner and Saint

David provides the Old Testament's best-known example of God showing love to a sinner. David is called a man after God's own heart, and yet he committed some of the most blatant and deliberate sins recorded in Scripture. When we read the account of David's sins in 2 Samuel, it seems hard to believe that God could bless and continue to love such a sinful, devious man. After David planned and carried out the murder of Uriah and committed adultery with Uriah's wife, Bathsheba, his deeds are condemned in the simple statement: "But the thing David had done displeased the Lord" (2 Sam 11:27).

Later, Nathan the prophet rebukes David and promises God's grave judgment. "This is what the LORD says: 'Out of your own household I am going to bring calamity upon you. Before your very eyes I will take your wives and give them to one who is close to you, and he will lie with your wives in broad daylight. You did it in secret, but I will do this thing in broad daylight before all Israel.' Then David said to Nathan, 'I have sinned against the LORD.' Nathan replied, 'The LORD has taken away your sin. You are not going to die' " (2 Sam 12:11-13).

This passage reveals several striking points: The magnitude of David's disobedience is confirmed by the way God chooses to respond to it. The child born to Bathsheba as a result of David's adultery dies when it is only days old (2 Sam 12:14-18). Further, while his adultery was done in secret, his wives would be taken in adultery for the whole city to see (2 Sam 16:20-23). And there was more—rebellion against David from his own household and the death of other sons. David does not get away with murder. His sin is great and God's judgment is equally severe.

But the story does not end here. David confesses in a single, profound yet simple sentence. And God's forgiveness is so available that Nathan quickly assures David that his sin has been removed and that his own life will be spared.

In a very real sense it is only in the presence of such grave sin that the immensity of God's love can be understood. David's understanding of this love is highlighted in Psalm 103: "As a father has compassion on his children, so the LORD has compassion on those who fear him; for he knows how we are formed, he remembers that we are dust. As for man, his days are like grass, he flourishes like a flower of the field; the wind blows over it and it is gone, and its place remembers it no more. But from everlasting to everlasting the LORD's love is with those who fear him" (Ps 103:13-17).

David's sin had brought him face to face with his feeble humanity. He sees how he is like dust that is blown away or like a flower that blooms and is gone. David's repentance brought David face to face with God's constant (from everlasting to everlasting) love.

"Who am I, O Sovereign LORD, and what is my family, that you have brought me this far?" David prays after hearing God's promises for victory over his enemies (2 Sam 7:18). David recognized God as sovereign—above everything. He was also a man who loved to praise God. "How great you are, O Sovereign LORD! There is no one like you, and there is no God but you, as we have heard with our own ears" (2 Sam 7:22).

Humility, the ability to praise and to recognize God's sovereignty gave David a solid foundation on which to build his life. David capped off his prayer with a great proclamation: "O Sovereign LORD, you are God! Your words are trustworthy, and you have given this good promise to your servant. Now be pleased to bless the house of your servant, that it may continue forever in your sight; for you, O Sovereign LORD, have spoken, and with your blessing the house of your servant will be blessed forever" (2 Sam 7:28-29). David acknowledges God's trustworthiness and asks for his blessing.

Suffice it to say David knew God. Fortunately for David he had such a sound base that when he did sin he turned back to God for forgiveness and new direction rather than turning away from God and into the garbage can of his mind. The result? God's forgiveness and the continuation of his love being lavished upon David.

The Love Theme of God's Forgiveness

How was David able to turn so quickly to God after such deliberate disobedience? He carried deep within him a great knowledge of God. Let's look at several love themes David sung of his God throughout his life.

Somehow it seems paradoxical to emphasize sin in order to cover it up. But that is exactly how confession and forgiveness work. We make the problem worse by ignoring our disobedience. We solve it by acknowledging it. This was precisely David's experience after he sinned. "Blessed is he whose transgressions are forgiven, whose sins are covered. Blessed is the man whose sin the LORD does not count against him and in whose spirit is no deceit. When I kept silent, my bones wasted away through my groaning all day long. For day and night your hand was heavy upon me; my strength was sapped as in the heat of summer. Then I acknowledged my sin to you and did not cover up my iniquity. I said, 'I will confess my transgressions to the LORD'—and you forgave the guilt of my sin" (Ps 32:1-5).

David experienced forgiveness in two important ways. First, his sin was covered and not counted against him. It takes a loving God to do that. God loved David enough (and he loves us enough) to completely clear him of the charges of sin brought against him. Other people often hold back their love and continue to remind us of our sin.

Not God. His love is so great he wants us to be complete-ly free from the burden. David knew this and knew it well.

Another result of God's forgiveness is freedom from guilt. It is one thing to be completely exonerated of our sin before God. It is another to accept God's love and forgiveness so completely that we no longer hold our sin against ourselves. God is not through dealing with our sin until he has restored us to complete peace. People who hold on to the guilt of their sin do not feel his blessing.

David knew that our loving God wants to do more for us. He wants to make us free again—free from our guilt so that we can unreservedly return his love. When we focus on God and his love, we grow. When we focus on sin—past, present or future—we stagnate and feel pow-erless. Guilt is a great impediment to Christian growth because it blinds us to God's complete acceptance of us. The way God shows his love to sinners is primarily by providing forgiveness and removing our guilt so the flow of his love can be restored to us.

The Love Theme of God's Mercy

God, of course, is not compelled to do anything for sinners. He could snuff us out like a candle if he wanted to. Looking back on our sin, however, helps us to realize that God chooses to forgive. We receive God's mercy when we do not get what we deserve.

When I have experienced God's love and mercy after I've sinned, God has brought to mind words from the writer of Lamentations: "Because of the Lord's great love we are not consumed" (Lam 3:22). When I first pondered this verse I was impressed with God's love and mercy in not destroying me in response to my sin. Certainly if it were not for his love and mercy, he would do so. He loves us too much to ignore our sin, and he loves us too much not to respond to our sin with compassion. It is only the hardness of our hearts and our refusal to repent which brings God's harsh judgment on us.

Not only can God's wrath consume me, so can my own choice to follow sin rather than to follow God. But his great love and mercy protect me from my own tendency to self-destruct. God's mercy is shown both in protection from the wages of sin and in protection from the powerful influence of sin in our lives daily.

It is little wonder that the writer went on to say, "for his compassions never fail. They are new every morning; great is your faithfulness. I say to myself, 'The LORD is my portion; therefore I will wait for him'" (Lam 3:22-24).

When David prayed for God's mercy in his great cry of repentance, Psalm 51, he did so with the awareness of three things—God's unfailing love, God's great compassion, and God's ability to blot out and wash away his sin: "Have mercy on me, O God, according to your unfailing love; according to your great compassion blot out my transgressions. Wash away all my iniquity and cleanse me from my sin" (Ps 51:1-2).

David focused on God's love and compassion rather than his own sin. He believed it was blotted out and washed away. This left David free to look ahead to what God had in store for him next. Sin should never be allowed to become the focal point in our lives. We need to follow David's example and focus our attention on the love and mercy which takes us beyond our sin to a new place of usefulness.

The Love Theme of God's Deliverance

David also prayed for deliverance. When he wrote a song of deliverance it was usually with one of two things in mind—deliverance from his outward enemies such as King Saul, or deliverance from his inward enemies such as his sin, his guilt or his capacity for evil.

In Psalm 25 David prayed, "Guard my life and rescue me; let me not be put to shame, for I take refuge in you. May integrity and uprightness protect me, because my hope is in you" (Ps 25:20-21). David was concerned about being overtaken by his enemies as well as being sidetracked by himself. Earlier in the psalm he emphasized his inward needs: "Show me your ways, O LORD, teach me your paths; guide me in your truth and teach me, for you are God my Savior, and my hope is in you all day long. Remember, O LORD, your great mercy and love, for they are from of old" (Ps 25:4-6).

I believe David had just as much confidence in God's ability to deliver him from his internal foes as from his external ones. David was set on God's love. In fact, David saw outward deliverance and inward deliverance as closely linked, one being as important as the other. "Rescue me from my enemies, O LORD, for I hide myself in you. Teach me to do your will, for you are my God; may your good Spirit lead me on level ground" (Ps 143:9-10). When David prayed to be led to level ground, he knew that God expected him to get walking. God wouldn't deliver him to the edge of a dangerous cliff or to the bottom of a deep pit. God always delivers us to something better. So his proper response, as is ours, is obedience to his will.

Likewise we can enjoy God's benefits. "He gives his king great victories; he shows unfailing kindness to his anointed, to David and his descendants forever" (Ps

18:50). God gave his king, David, great victories. As his descendants we need not expect anything less.

The Love Theme of God's Goodness

The word David used most often to describe God's goodness was the noun *toob*. It can be easily translated "the best." David was saying, "God, you are the best to me. Whether I see it in the beauty, good things or joy you give, God, you are the best." As David exclaimed, "How great is your goodness, which you have stored up for those who fear you, which you bestow in the sight of men on those who take refuge in you" (Ps 31:19).

David is saying that God really knows how to treat his children. God is extravagant. He pours it on!

In Psalm 33 the same word for goodness has been translated "unfailing love" in the New International Version. God's love is unfailing day by day. As David prayed in Psalm 23, "Surely goodness and love will follow me all the days of my life, and I will dwell in the house of the LORD forever" (Ps 23:6).

It is one thing to revel in God's love when we are in need of forgiveness or deliverance from ourselves or others. However, we are much poorer if we fail to see God's goodness and revel in his love day after day, in the ordinary ups and downs of life.

The Love Theme of God's Generosity

God is also the great giver—even to sinners. David recognized this. "The LORD gives strength to his people; the LORD blesses his people with peace" (Ps 29:11).

I am slowly learning that if I want strength, I have to look to the strong one. If I want peace, I need to look to the source of peace. It's not that God is stingy. Rather,

I usually try to find strength and peace elsewhere before I open the packages God has put under my tree.

When Paul wrote to the Philippians from prison it is obvious that he had sampled God's gifts to him: "Rejoice in the Lord always. I will say it again: Rejoice! Let your gentleness be evident to all. The Lord is near. Do not be anxious about anything, but in everything, by prayer and petition, with thanksgiving, present your requests to God. And the peace of God, which transcends all understanding, will guard your hearts and your minds in Christ Jesus" (Phil 4:4-7). He had strength to survive in the midst of adversity, and he obviously had peace. The Lord is near and so are his gifts.

David also experienced God's giving when the going was tough. "Unless the LORD had given me help, I would soon have dwelt in the silence of death. When I said, 'My foot is slipping,' your love, O LORD, supported me. When anxiety was great within me, your consolation brought joy to my soul" (Ps 94:17-19).

God helped David. He spared his life. He supported him. He even consoled him and brought him joy when he was tremendously worried. David was able to receive these gifts, I think, because he understood a God who wants to give and he waited long enough to receive. Have you ever become impatient and run off before God's gifts to you had time to arrive?

God's gifts are both physical and emotional—a total sense of well-being. As another psalmist wrote, "For the LORD God is a sun and shield; the LORD bestows favor and honor; no good thing does he withhold from those whose walk is blameless" (Ps 84:11). These verses underscore the breadth and completeness of God's giving ("no good thing does he withhold").

A discussion of God's gifts would be incomplete without Psalm 37:4: "Delight yourself in the LORD and he will give you the desires of your heart." This verse has been a source of great hope and comfort for some and great consternation for others. Certainly the thought of God giving us the desires of our hearts is most welcome. No one else can promise that. God loves me so much that he even cares about the desires of my heart. Even more amazing, he even wants to give me those desires.

The consternation comes when I realize that God has not given me *everything* I wanted or desired. He did not heal my father-in-law whom I loved very much. He has not done everything I have asked him to do for my children. He hasn't even taken away all the rough spots in my relationship with my wife. What's the matter, Lord? Where are you when I need you?

A single friend who desires marriage also needs you. She has prayed for more than ten years. Are you going to give her the desire of her heart? I know that you know what's best for us, Lord, but not all of our unmet desires seem to be out of line.

Some of the struggles which come from reading a promise such as this can be answered by considering more carefully what the Scripture actually says. The command to delight in the Lord comes in the middle of several commands in this psalm. Others include: do not fret; trust in the Lord; commit your way to the Lord; be still before the Lord; and refrain from anger. When the command has a promise attached to it, the two are closely related.

What is the command associated with being given the desires of our heart? "Delight yourself." The word for "delight" means to be soft and pliable. We might say be moldable or teachable. It means more than being happy or excited about God.

Next, consider the meaning of *heart*. The Hebrews used this word to denote both our feelings and our intellect. It is our central being. In other words, it is the desires most central to our being that God promises to give. It strikes me, that if I am soft and pliable before the Lord, he will have a great deal to do with the formation of those central desires. In other words, I will be like David—a man after God's own heart. He will give me the things that flow out of his character. These may be much different from what I might naturally desire. The emphasis is on developing inward qualities rather than manipulating circumstances.

What are desires? There are two different Hebrew words which are translated "desire." One appears in Psalm 140:8: "Do not grant the wicked their desires, O LORD." David is asking God not to give the wicked their lustful or covetous desires. Compare this with Ephesians 2:3-5: "All of us also lived among them at one time, gratifying the cravings of our sinful nature and following its *desires* and thoughts. Like the rest, we were by nature objects of wrath. But because of his great love for us, God, who is rich in mercy, made us alive with Christ even when we were dead in transgressions—it is by grace you have been saved."

God's love provides a transition from evil desires to the desires that are a part of our new life in Christ. Psalm 37 is talking about the desires of a changed life, a life which is pliable in God's hands. This may or may not rule out some of our natural desires such as for marriage or for God's best for our children or our marriage. God does give those things as well. I believe, however, that the major promise of the passage is that as we stay soft and pliable before the Lord, he meets our central desire which is safety and security in our awareness of his love for us.

Paul wrote, "For Christ's love compels us, because we are convinced that one dies for all, and therefore all died. And he died for all, that those who live should no longer live for themselves but for him who died for them and was raised again" (2 Cor 5:14-15). One of God's greatest gifts to us is the change from our selfish orientation to God's orientation. We need it and we want it, but sometimes we miss it when we do not delight ourselves in the Lord.

The Love Theme of God's Faithfulness

Jim spoke out strongly, "I want to believe all this stuff about God and his love, but frankly I just don't know if he can be trusted." Jim grew up not knowing whether or not anyone could be trusted. These feelings intensified when Jim violated family standards. He thought his family would turn their backs on him if they found out what he'd done. Sin undermines our belief in the faithfulness of others, even in our belief in God's faithfulness.

How did David, the sinner, survive after his sin? In his psalm of repentance, Psalm 51, David refers to God's "unfailing love." Apparently David still had a grasp of the faithfulness of God on a personal basis. In Psalm 57 he writes, "God sends his love and his faithfulness. . . . For great is your love, reaching to the heavens; your faithfulness reaches to the skies" (Ps 57:3, 10). The greatest love is the love that is always there. You can count on it. "Your love, O LORD, reaches to the heavens, your faithfulness to the skies" (Ps 36:5). God's love and faithfulness are locked together. "I will sing of the love of the LORD's great love forever; with my mouth I will make your faithfulness known through all generations" (Ps 89:1).

God's faithfulness is mentioned at least seven times in Psalm 89. The psalmist doesn't want to leave any doubt about it. Our loving God is faithful.

But what if we do sin? What can we expect from God at those times? Ethan the psalmist spoke to that point as well: "I will punish their sin with the rod, their iniquity with flogging; but I will not take my love from him, nor will I ever betray my faithfulness" (Ps 89:32-33). God's reaction to our sin may be punishment if punishment is necessary, but it will never be the removal of his love. To stop loving us, to be unfaithful to us, is outside the character of God.

Not even sin can stop God from loving. Sin can only stop us from receiving God's great love. No wonder Paul wrote, "Who shall separate us from the love of Christ? Shall trouble or hardship or persecution or famine or nakedness or danger or sword? . . . No, in all these things we are more than conquerors through him who loved us. For I am convinced that neither death nor life, neither angels nor demons, neither the present nor the future, nor any powers, neither height nor depth, nor anything else in all creation, will be able to separate us from the love of God that is in Christ Jesus our Lord" (Rom 8:35, 37-39).

Writing about the love themes from the life of David, the sinner, could be a lifelong project. The list goes on and on. We have not written of God's saving power, his trustworthiness, his justice, righteousness or his power to heal. Suffice it to say that you cannot exhaust the love of God and David knew it so well.

When my daughter was young we used to play the How Much Game.

"Does God love me this much?" she would ask as she parted her hands.

"Yes," I would reply.

"This much?" she would ask, parting her hands even further.

"Yes," I said.

"How about this much?" she asked with her arms extended to either side.

Once again I replied yes.

One day she said, "Does God love me that much even when I'm bad?"

I replied, "Yes, he does."

She just looked at me in amazement and said, "Wow!"

5

UNDERSTANDING THE SOURCE OF LOVE

 M att *is sixteen. He has been living on the street for* two years. He says he is tired. But he isn't talking about being weary. He's talking about being too old to make money as a male prostitute. When he first came to the Green House (a home for throwaway and runaway children), he noticed some strange behavior on the part of the staff. He saw them doing things for other people without expecting anything in return. He was skeptical, untrusting and full of questions. He didn't have any categories for understanding such behavior because up until then all he had known was using and being used. Love for him was a word you said to get a place to sleep or to earn enough money to keep you alive for another day. "People don't love," he said. "They only use you to get what they want."

Matt's appraisal of the world is all too accurate. The majority of people do use others to get what they want. Sadly, the kind of behavior he saw in the staff at the Green House is not typical. It seems to spring from a different source. Matt was curious about such a difference. He was tired—tired of being used. He needed a love that would accept and understand him. He needed a love that would bring healing to his used body and soul.

When I was young my father would say, "You can't get blood out of a turnip." He was trying to help me understand that everything has a source, and if you want something, you have to go to the source. You can't get love from someone who doesn't have it. At best you will get a counterfeit. And there is counterfeit love—people trying to get their own needs met under the guise of meeting the needs of others. Matt knew all about this counterfeit. In fact, he didn't know there was anything else. If you can't get blood out of a turnip and you can't find love in the home or on the street, then where do you go? Obviously, you must go to the source. God's love can't be counterfeit love, because he has no needs. He is totally self-sufficient. And we can love because he makes us sufficient.

He Is the Source

Matt could tell that the people at the house were different. He had a strange feeling that if there was such a thing as love, they were close to it. He began to ask questions about their behavior. He watched their every move. He was looking for something that he wasn't even sure existed. In essence he was trying to trace love back to its source. His search was shortened by an amazing statement in a timeless book—"Whoever does not love does not know God, because God is love" (1 Jn 4:8).

Matt's experience had brought him into contact with hundreds of people who did not love. It was easy for him to believe that they didn't know God. What he hadn't encountered was people who could love. "How come they are different?" he asked. "Can they be trusted?"

God is love. It is his nature. He can reach out and meet our needs. We are so wrapped up in trying to survive that we cannot consider the needs of others. God is self-sufficient and therefore capable of meeting our needs, capable of showing us love. Love flows from the strength of God. Only God is love. He is the essence of love. People can express love, but he is the only source. When we receive his love, we become sufficient to give love to others.

C. S. Lewis wrote, "The loves prove that they are unworthy to take the place of God by the fact that they cannot even remain themselves and do what they promise to do without God's help."[1]

Although love is impossible apart from the source, there is hope for those who want to be loving people. God wants to develop our capacity to love. In fact, he shows us love so we can pass it on to others. The more we pass it on the more we become like the source.

God is in the process of expanding his love to the whole world. He is the source. One response to God's love is to be able to love. "We love because he first loved us" (1 Jn 4:19). As we receive love from the source, we in turn become energized to reach out in love to others. "God has poured out his love into our hearts by the Holy Spirit, whom he has given us" (Rom 5:5).

Let me underscore what it means to be loved by someone who is not dependent on our love to sustain his own ability to love. In chapter one we read part of Paul's description of love in 1 Corinthians 13. Consider its description of love again—patient, kind, not jealous, not boastful. It is very difficult to act this way if our own needs aren't met. When you feel a need to be loved, how patient are you? Does your kindness hold out? Are you envious of others who seem to be receiving the love you desire? When you receive a little love do you want to boastfully tell everyone about it?

Only the source of love is capable of not being self-serving. Our insecurities and defenses undermine love. We don't trust the love of others because we don't trust ourselves. Yet we desperately need love to be assured of our worth. Thus love becomes manipulated. The more we strive to insure love, the more angry and calculating we become. Even small children play the game. "Mommy loves me more than she does you." Or, "You got into trouble and Daddy is going to be angry with you. He doesn't love you anymore." The brutality continues on. Where will it end?

It ends where the source of love begins. For love "always protects, always trusts, always hopes, always perseveres" (1 Cor 13:7). Love flows out of completeness. God is alone complete. The closer we get to the source of love, the more we are able to give up the negatives associated with striving for our own completeness—unkindness, envy, boastfulness and the like. We become loving people because the source of love indwells us, and we become secure in that love.

Love and Acceptance

Eugene Kennedy wrote a book with the intriguing title, _If You Really Knew Me, Would You Still Like Me?_ It is hard to receive love when we don't feel accepted. Fortunately, the source of love doesn't have this problem. God is totally acceptable to himself and therefore has no trouble receiving our love. Acceptance of self and others frees us to give and receive love.

We can find this freedom when we savor the fact that the source of love knows us and loves us dearly. J. I. Packer writes,

> He knows me as a friend, one who loves me; and there is no moment when His eye is off me, or His attention distracted from me, and no moment, therefore, when His care falters.
>
> This is momentous knowledge. There is unspeakable comfort—the sort of comfort that energizes, be it said, not enervates—in knowing that God is constantly taking knowledge of me in love, and watching over me for my good. There is tremendous relief in knowing that His love to me is utterly realistic, based at every point on prior knowledge of the worst about me, so that no discovery now can disillusion him about me.[2]

God's acceptance of us becomes the electrical conduit through which love can flow from the hydroelectrical plant to you and me the substation, and on to the individual lights we may contact.

God the source of love accepts you and me. That is a great word of encouragement. John Powell writes:

> In the Old Testament God reveals himself to the people of Israel as a God of unconditional love. His gift of himself in the choice and creation of "My People" is totally unsolicited, undeserved and unmerited. In the seventh chapter of Deuteronomy it is very clear that God's love for his people was not based on any-

thing they were or had. The Hebrew word used to describe this kind of covenanted and unconditional love is *hesed*. It can be translated as "loving kindness," but *hesed* clearly implies that this love is an unmerited gift and an irrevocable commitment. God decides, God chooses, God offers his gift of love. He is by his own free act forever committed to his people.[3]

Love's Transforming Character

When we speak of God as the source of love we are led to ask, "What does that mean to me?" The answer is, it changes us. We are transformed. How this takes place is found in 1 John 3. Let's look at it piece by piece.

Verse 1 begins, "How great is the love the Father has lavished on us, that we should be called children of God! And that is what we are!" We are not only loved; we have become family. We are his own flesh and blood, as it were. We take on the very nature of God. The transformation begins with a new birth. We are born into the family of love. How do we become family? God claims us. He says, "You are mine. I have chosen to love you." This is not something we grasp intellectually. It is only as we relate to God our Father, who is lavishing his love on us, that we really understand just how remarkable it is. God loves me and that is exciting. God loves you. When the excitement of his love soaks in, it changes us dramatically.

The next phase of our transformation is seen in verse two. Our potential is not yet realized. "What we will be has not been made known." So much of our thinking today is negative. We expect the worst. We expect to fail. We expect to fall apart. We expect to die. We expect to be miserable.

But the emphasis in verse 2 is positive. Some great things are about to happen. We are becoming like the source of love. As this happens joy begins to take the place of drudgery.

Have you ever noticed the difference between having to do something and getting to do something? My son Mike is not too fond of household chores. But he likes his piano teacher a great deal. They get along famously. So even though he is not particularly domestic, he gladly volunteered to help serve refreshments at a recital. It was a labor of love. Loving becomes easier because of love.

I have met many people who seem to be waiting to get to heaven to become the people they would like to be. Why wait? The potential for becoming more loving is now. I become more like the source of love as I love others by faith. I must trust God to show me how to love, even when I don't feel like it, if I want to grow. Faith is the means by which I collect the promise God has made—"We shall be like him, for we shall see him as he is" (v. 2).

At a church meeting I watched Bill being unnecessarily attacked by another member with a critical spirit. Bill quietly listened, asked questions of his assailant and softly corrected some erroneous statements. What he did not do was take advantage of the opportunities he had to tear into his accuser. He left the other person whole, even though he could have done otherwise. As a result of Bill's loving choices, healing was brought to the assailant and to the local church body. Later that evening I told Bill how much I appreciated seeing him exhibit some of his potential for love. Bill and I both knew that he hadn't always been capable of such love. He smiled at me and said, "It is rather amazing. God is at work—even in me."

In 1 John 3:3-9 we see another consequence of staying close to the source of love. "Everyone who has this hope in him purifies himself, just as he is pure" (v. 3). The more we are touched by God's love the more we want to be like him. I have met so many people who are afraid of God. They know that their lives are impure and so they are afraid of getting close to God for fear that he will give them what they deserve—severe punishment. Does God always deal with our sin and impurity through punishment? I don't think so. My experience has been that when I have drifted from God, he has drawn me back by showing me special love. He has answered a prayer I was almost too ashamed to pray, or he has used me in the life of another person. I have been humbled by his great expressions of love when I absolutely knew I didn't deserve it. This realization has brought me to repentance and back to the source of love.

God does not delight in punishing. He delights in loving. That is who he is. God punishes only when we refuse to draw near to him and accept his love. When we sin we tend to become fearful of God and to hide. We learned that from our forefathers.

> Then the man and his wife heard the sound of the LORD God as he was walking in the garden in the cool of the day, and they hid from the LORD God among the trees of the garden. But the LORD God called to the man, "Where are you?"
>
> He answered, "I heard you in the garden, and I was afraid because I was naked; so I hid."
>
> And he said, "Who told you that you were naked? Have you eaten from the tree that I commanded you

not to eat from?" (Gen 3:8-11)

The more we hide the more obscure the source of love seems to us. The solution is to decide to run toward God not away from him. Approach leads to repentance, and repentance leads to purity and a greater ability to receive and give love. If we wait to approach the source of love until after we have started living a better life, we will never get there. God changes us as we approach him. It is a step of faith.

Many times I have cried, "God I don't understand why you choose to love me and to bless me when I am so disobedient. But I want to thank you for that love and ask you to cleanse me and help me to get back on the path—and stay there." In this way I identify strongly with the wayward son.

> So he got up and went to his father.
>
> But while he was still a long way off, his father saw him and was filled with compassion for him; he ran to his son, threw his arms around him and kissed him.
>
> The son said to him, "Father, I have sinned against heaven and against you. I am no longer worthy to be called your son."
>
> But the father said to his servants, "Quick! Bring the best robe and put it on him. Put a ring on his finger and sandals on his feet. Bring the fattened calf and kill it. Let's have a feast and celebrate. For this son of mine was dead and is alive again; he was lost and is found. So they began to celebrate. (Lk 15:20-24)

The father forgave before the son confessed his wrong-doing. He responded to the son's movement in the right direction. When the son was still a long way off, he ran to embrace him. Even when the son does state his guilt, the father virtually ignores it, so great is his joy at seeing the son he loved alive again. He knows the boy is no longer worthy to be called his son. But he also knows his son would be too ashamed to return for any other reason than to confess his sin. The father is so ready to forgive that he ignores his son's words and rushes to restore him to his full status in the family and begin the celebration.

God does not give me what I deserve either. If he did, I would have been extinguished long ago. This overwhelms me. He rushes to forgive me with outstretched arms. Thinking about this great love leads me to purity because it makes me want to be like him.

Contact with the source of love not only leads to changes in our response to God but also changes in our responses to others. "Anyone who does not do what is right is not a child of God; nor is anyone who does not love his brother" (1 Jn 3:10). Neither doing what is right nor loving others is natural for fallen human beings. Such actions are the result of being born of God. God's love can change our self-centeredness into a desire to love and do what is right. The sacrificial death of Christ for us makes it all possible. Paul wrote, "We implore you on Christ's behalf: Be reconciled to God. God made him who had no sin to be sin for us, so that in him we might become the righteousness of God" (2 Cor 5:20-21).

As a child I especially remember how hard it was to do what was right. It was always easier to do what I felt like doing instead of what my parents wanted me to do. I needed to be changed by the source of love so that I in turn could love and choose the right. Now that I am a parent, I see my children struggling with the same issue. In one way or another all of my children have said, "Being good is hard."

Is there anything that makes right living and right

loving easier? Yes! Staying close to the source of love. It was always easier to obey my parents when I was close to them. They encouraged me and smiled when I followed their desires. It was when I withdrew from their presence that I was tempted to go my own way. It is true that I had to learn to think for myself and to make my own decisions, but my awareness of the constant love of my parents cleared the path for this step of growth.

Staying close to the source of love also helps us to escape from death to life. This may sound strange. Maybe we don't think of ourselves as death oriented. But notice carefully what John says: "Do not be surprised, my brothers, if the world hates you. We know that we have passed from death to life, because we love our brothers. Anyone who does not love remains in death" (1 Jn 3:13-14). Because of our fearful self-protectiveness, we do not naturally respond to others out of love. Being able to love others is one of the evidences of God's love for you. In other words, we are changed from a death orientation (wanting to hurt others) to a love orientation (wanting to see others prosper). Why is there so much hate in the world? The answer is quite simple. Because there is so little love. God wants us to draw close to him so that he can do something about that. The worst thing about our hate is not so much what it does to others but what it does to us. It consumes us like a fire consumes a beautiful tree. We need to constantly be looking for ways to help each other avoid the hate trap. As Paul says, "Fathers, do not exasperate your children" (Eph 6:4). Likewise consider the remarkable statement Jesus made in the Sermon on the Mount: "Therefore, if you are offering your gift at the altar and there remember that your brother has something against you, leave your gift there in front of the altar. First go and be reconciled to your brother; then come and offer your gift" (Mt 5:23-24).

Why should one allow worship to be interrupted just to straighten things out with a brother? Obviously because God said so. But why would he say so? The context of the statement is a discussion of hate and murder. Jesus was just explaining how anger is creating murder in your heart. Obviously this is not pleasing to God. Therefore in the passage Jesus is saying, "You can do something to help a brother or sister to avoid this sin. If you know that they are angry toward you, get up from the altar and get things straightened out. I will be worshiped by your action which may enable them to leave their sin of mental murder and therefore transform them from death to life." It is a wonderful thing to be able to love another person by releasing them from their anger. Staying close to the source of love will keep us open to the needs of others.

After preaching a sermon on reconciliation I invited the congregation to go to people they were separated from and to ask for or give forgiveness. One man said afterward, "I have been released from my anger, and besides that I now have my brother back." Take the risk of trying to love in this way. You will find God faithful in supplying you with his resources.

Staying close to the source of love results in another change in the loved person. John writes, "This is how we know what love is: Jesus Christ laid down his life for us. And we ought to lay down our lives for our brothers. If anyone has material possessions and sees his brother in need but has no pity on him, how can the love of God be in him? Dear children, let us not love with words or tongue but with actions and in truth" (1 Jn 3:16-18).

God as the source of love enables us to engage in sacrificial acts of love for those around us. The paramount example of sacrificial love is Christ's death for us. We are led by this example to risk our lives for others and to give until it hurts. It is a strong challenge but in reality it is what loving is all about.

Ted gave up his noon racquetball game for six weeks to meet with John, a new believer. Granted it didn't cost Ted his life but loving always costs something. When I asked Ted how he felt about his sacrifice, he said, "At first I couldn't believe that I had agreed to do it. Later on, I was as excited to meet with John as I had been to play racquetball." When we extend ourselves to others in love, God is faithful to touch us anew with his greater love.

Calvin Miller wrote, "Love is the essence of Christian meaning, but its meaning is always imbedded in mystery. God's love is far above all human understanding. Like its existence its constancy does not depend upon reason either."[4]

To be loving we must stay in touch with the source of love.

6

LOVE AS A LIFESTYLE

To feel loved we must undergo some drastic changes. This is the clear implication of the chapter on savoring. One basic change is a decision to focus on the many ways God loves us. This is essential if we are to savor God's love. What might be less obvious but just as real is that such a decision could lead to an entire new way of living.

As Christians we shouldn't be surprised at this. Jesus himself called us to be different from the way most people choose to live. We are to be a holy, or a "set apart," people. Followers of Jesus are to carry the message of God's love into the schools and factories and offices and neighborhoods of our world. Love is to become our lifestyle. It is to be our witness to the world of the great love

God has for us. "By this will all men know that you are my disciples, if you love one another" (Jn 13:35).

I don't know about you, but expressing love isn't always my strong suit. It is much easier for me to talk about love or write about love than it is to get down to the everyday business of loving. John challenges us to get on with the task, "Dear children, let us not love with words or tongue but with actions and in truth" (1 Jn 3:18).

Prerequisites to Love as a Lifestyle

Before you sign up for "Love as a Lifestyle 101," it may help to check the course catalog to see if you have the required prerequisites. Some are listed in John 15:9-13: "As the Father has loved me, so have I loved you. Now remain in my love. If you obey my commands, you will remain in my love, just as I have obeyed my Father's commands and remain in his love. I have told you this so that my joy may be in you and that your joy may be complete. My command is this: Love each other as I have loved you. Greater love has no one than this, that he lay down his life for his friends."

The first prerequisite is persistence. Three times in the above passage we are told to "remain in" his love. To love like the Master, you need to stay under the Master's love. It boils down to staying close enough to the Lord to experience his love and pass it on.

Why is remaining so important? Because sometimes after we have received generously from God we feel we can give forever without being revitalized. This is just not so. As soon as we begin to remove ourselves from Christ (thinking that we know how to be loving on our own), his love grows dim in us. God doesn't charge our love batteries permanently. He made us to be charged daily or hourly as we stay close to him.

The issue is fellowship. God wants us to fellowship with him, and in doing so he enables us to love. This prerequisite doesn't sound too difficult. But we all have a strong tendency to want to do things our own way. Remaining takes discipline.

The second prerequisite concerns the quality of love we are willing to commit ourselves to. Obviously there are many different standards of love we could choose to follow. God's design, however, is quite specific: "Love each other as I have loved you." God's model of love is sacrifice. We must likewise be willing to give ourselves to others. If we are not willing to give up something to love another person, we are probably not loving at all.

Sometimes I get concerned when I see my wife inconveniencing herself so much to reach out to people with her love. I am worried that she might overextend herself. And at times I have become angry when these people aren't even willing to love enough in return to make Sandy's life a little easier. Then I remember that giving your life for another is a prerequisite to loving. Slowly I have learned that part of loving is not to expect something in return.

A third prerequisite is to decide which world we will live in. Love as a lifestyle can't be divided between two worlds. John wrote, "Do not love the world or anything in the world. If anyone loves the world, the love of the Father is not in him. For everything in the world—the cravings of sinful man, the lust of his eyes and the boasting of what he has and does—comes not from the Father but from the world. The world and its desires pass away, but the man who does the will of God lives forever" (1

Jn 2:15-17).

Choice is a necessary part of loving. We only have so much energy and we have to decide where we are going to invest it. We are tempted to put our love into false or unproductive things. The pleasures of this life seem so desirable. The truth, however, is that pleasure seekers don't have time to love.

Donald spends so much of his time seeking the approval of others that he has no time to give approval to those he could love. Maxine is trying so hard to do what makes her feel good that she doesn't exercise the opportunity to bring joy to others.

If I sound like I'm coming down hard on pleasure, let me explain. I'm not suggesting that we try to rid our lives of all pleasure. Even if this were possible, it would not accomplish God's purpose. He himself gives us pleasure and wants us to enjoy the things around us. The distinction is one of lifestyle. Are we living for pleasure with loving as a sideline? Or is love our lifestyle with pleasure as a delightful addition?

We can best answer these questions by looking at how we spend our time. Sometimes keeping track of the actual minutes and hours we spend at various activities can be a real eye opener. Sometimes even a minor adjustment can make an enormous difference in our life. If you watch TV for pleasure ten hours per week, for example, just think how God might use three of those hours if you made them available to do household repairs for a widow, visit a prisoner, tutor an illiterate person, lead a neighborhood Bible study, start a prayer chain or organize meals for a family with a hospitalized parent.

The little choices we make now add up to big choices. They shape us as inevitably as making a major commitment. As John Powell says, "What you and I will become in the end will be just more and more of what we are deciding and trying to be right now. There is a fundamental choice, a life principle, which will one day possess us in the marrow of our bones and by the blood in our veins. It is a certainty that we will die as we have lived."[1] Love needs to become a habit.

The Course Work
We've hit the prerequisites. What do we learn in the course itself? We start with the flip side of one of the prerequisites. The positive half of being willing to sacrifice for others is giving. Giving can become a joyful habit. Giving cards, giving small gifts, giving time, giving kind words—it can become so much a part of our lives that we are more concerned about giving than receiving.

Giving for the sake of another is an inspiring way to live. It is like planting a seed. It may appear dead for a time, but then it grows into a new life.

This habit of giving may be misunderstood because we have been trained to think that no one really gives unless he or she is out to get something in return. In reality Christians do expect something in return. We expect a new quality of life. The vitality for this life, however, does not come from the person to whom we give but from the God for whom we give. Only he gives life. "Whoever finds his life will lose it, and whoever loses his life for my sake will find it" (Mt 10:39).

The second thing we learn in the course of love as lifestyle concerns the recipients of our love. It is easy for us to love some people. Friends and family need love, and they are often easy to love. Loving just these people, however, will not meet God's total plan. Notice what

Jesus told us to do in the Sermon on the Mount: "You have heard that it was said, 'Love your neighbor and hate your enemy.' But I tell you: Love your enemies and pray for those who persecute you, that you may be sons of your Father in heaven" (Mt 5:43-45).

Jesus' great challenge to love extends beyond our comfort zones. And many of us have narrow comfort zones. Being an occupant of planet Earth means we will interact with a cross section of humanity—those we are naturally inclined to love, those we don't know well enough to love or to hate, and those we are pretty sure we can't tolerate!

When love becomes our lifestyle we first find new ways to love those closest to us. Then we may be ready to take on the challenge of strangers. The first step may simply be a willingness to step out and be available to converse. As we are friendly, we may see new opportunities to love.

Joan said, "It was amazing! When I just took the risk of trying to show interest in other people I discovered that they needed to be loved. I didn't feel like I had a lot to give, but when I was willing to give I found that their demands were not greater than what God had prepared me to do. Before, I was afraid to step toward others because I was afraid I wouldn't know what to do or say."

What does it mean to love your enemies? Maybe it starts by trusting God to be your protector against the hurt that they might inflict on you. Sometimes it is like trying to feed an injured animal. The animal thinks you are its enemy because of its fear. It wants to hurt you to protect itself. Once you show your intentions the animosity may cease. One of the greatest challenges is to love even when your vulnerability may give the other person the advantage over you. Taking this risk can prove to the world that ultimately it is God whom we trust for our well-being and not just our own craftiness.

When a power struggle arises with a family member, I need to be honest enough to admit my weaknesses— even if the other person could take advantage of my admission. When I show that God can help me to be honest about myself, the other person is more open to the possibility that God can meet his or her need as well.

Third, we learn that love means action. Deeds not words dictate the lifestyle. We tend to talk too much and do too little. The result? Emptiness and feelings of guilt. Instead we should look for opportunities to love, not for opportunities to talk about loving. I find that the more I engage in loving deeds the more loving I feel. I can't change my behavior by talking. But when I do reach out and touch someone, I begin to feel more loving. Actions not only speak louder than words; they also change emotions more than words.

Marty got tired of being depressed and drawn within herself. She decided to go on what she called a love campaign. Instead of making lists of all the loving deeds she could do when she felt better, she began to do them. She recognized that we rarely love tomorrow. If it is going to get done, it better be today—even if we don't feel like it. Marty was able to get ninety per cent of the things done she wanted to do. And her energy level grew larger instead of smaller as she had previously predicted. Her depression lessened and she even reported that she felt more loved by others than she had for a long time. The campaign was a success.

One successful campaign doesn't make a lifestyle, but it is a beginning. I encouraged Marty to level out her efforts so that she wouldn't burn out and to make sure she continued her efforts regularly. It is the regularity that eventually changes into a lifestyle. We all love best when we love with both word and deed.

Last, love as lifestyle means giving and receiving forgiveness. Just because we are loving doesn't mean we are perfect. We will offend others even in our attempts to love. And even those who love us will hurt us from time to time. The only defense against such hurt is a willingness to forgive and to keep on loving. Think how many times Jesus was hurt even by those very close to him. Yet this did not stop him from showing his sacrificial love to them.

Hear Paul's strong words of encouragement: "Bear with each other and forgive whatever grievances you may have against one another. Forgive as the Lord forgave you. And over all these virtues put on love, which binds them all together in perfect unity" (Col 3:13-14).

The standard is high. We are to forbear and to forgive as Christ forgave us. Notice too that after Paul tells us to forgive he then says we should put on love. Usually we think of it the other way around: If I am loving, then I will forgive. But Paul seems to indicate that we can learn to love by first forgiving.

I have discovered that as soon as I decide to show Christ's love to others, I will either upset someone or get angry for what someone did to me. The enemy knows that such conflicts are great deterents to developing a loving lifestyle. If I can be stopped by my anger or by my unwillingness to forgive, then God's plan is sidetracked.

Forgiveness is not just for special occasions or for Communion Sunday. It is an attitude which must permeate us. It isn't surprising that Jesus said we are to be willing to forgive seventy times seven. It is this constant willingness to forgive which paves the way for a lifestyle of loving.

Putting It into Practice

What can be more frustrating than to take a course and get some new knowledge but then not know how to put it into practice? When it comes to loving, we can take some definite action.

Let's start at the top. I've said it before, but it's worth saying again. We start by recommitting ourselves to the source of love. The only way we can live love as a lifestyle is to stay close to God's love—enjoying it, savoring it, basking in it. God loves and he gives. We have the wonderful opportunity to receive and then to love. Loving as a lifestyle requires that we aggressively seek after God and joyfully receive the love he wants to lavish on us. As a friend said, "If you don't know that God loves you, you don't know God."

After recommitting ourselves to God's love, we then commit ourselves to love a particular person. The more concrete our desired behavior, the easier it is to practice. We cannot love everybody. Love requires much more precision than that. Love requires that we get to know the other person well enough to reach out and meet his or her particular needs.

Begin with one person and develop the habits and skills of loving. As you see God working through you, you will be better equipped to extend your loving lifestyle to a greater number of people. The point is to start someplace. Start small and do the best job possible. Then look for new opportunities to expand or increase your loving outreach.

A third way to implement a loving lifestyle is to reconcile a broken relationship. It doesn't matter who is to blame for the brokenness. God calls us to wholeness. Earlier we looked at Jesus' command in the Sermon on the Mount to be reconciled before we make an offering at the altar (Mt 5:23-24).

Not only is Jesus saying that reconciliation is a prerequisite to worship; it may also save the other person from committing murder against you in their hearts. For the context of these verses is the commandment, "Do not murder." As Christians we are charged to suppress hostility whenever possible. By seeking reconciliation you or I may love the person out of their hateful self-destructive attitudes.

Another step of implementation is to form a new friendship. Sometimes we are the most lonely people in the world because we are afraid of new relationships. We try to live out our Christianity as lone rangers, but God's way is always the way of fellowship. Love says I will be a friend and I will receive a friend.

I suggest we begin with fellow Christians because through this new relationship we can each learn more about our God. I need to know God in the special ways he makes himself known to you, and you need to know God as he has been revealed to me. All we have to do is take the risk of reaching out.

At the same time, friendships with those who do not know God are a vital way to show love. This is our fifth option. Most nonbelievers think that Christians are better than them or that Christians somehow feel that they are better. Both myths need to be attacked. We are not better—we are different. We have not become superior—we have been changed. We are a part of a new family, but it is not an exclusive family. In fact, God is constantly looking for new sons and daughters to adopt. We love as we let non-Christians get a glimpse of our new family and invite them to become a part of it. God's family is not a social club. It is an adoption agency, a place where all can belong and where all can be equal in importance even while remaining different in gifts, abilities and function. Friendship is not only one of the great ways of loving. It is also a great way to show people who God is.

Nonbelievers cry out to see love in action. They hear that God loves the world and they may even have been told that he loves them individually, but they haven't seen it in action. They need to see that we really do sacrifice for our fellow believers. They need to see that we are also willing to go out of our way for them. After all, who wants to get involved with a God whose followers are self-centered?

Learning to love as a life principle is learning to be like God so that others can see what he is like and then have courage enough to commit their lives to him. When we are willing to be loving, we become windows to God. We can be an example of what God is like. We can't be perfect examples. But God doesn't expect us to be. He just wants us to represent the family as well as we can.

The sixth way of implementing love as a lifestyle may seem strange because it requires us to draw limits. We need to limit relationships which are getting out of hand. Love must be able to say no as well as yes. If we are to reach out to a number of people, then we cannot be controlled by any one of them.

Bob's friend Phil would like Bob to spend time with him every day. Bob was willing, but Phil would completely monopolize all of his time. If Bob was going to continue to love Phil by spending time with him, then he had to put some structure on the situation. Bob concluded that something had to be done.

"Phil," he said, "I enjoy being with you and giving and receiving support, but we need some guidelines. When we get together I will specify how much time I can spare, and then I need you to help me to hold to my time limits. This will help me to enjoy our time together, and it will also help you not to form the habit of trying to control others." Phil didn't like it at first, but he learned that in the long run both parties benefited by Bob loving enough to set some controls on the relationship.

If you give into all the demands of the people you are trying to love, you will only train them to be the kind of people you hate. It is much better to be loving and giving and firm. We need to love people by calling them to be all they can be. In Phil's case he needed to be called to be respectful of Bob. Through Bob's tough love Phil became a more thoughtful and more respected member of the community. How tragic it would have been if Bob had been so timid that he had just given Phil everything he wanted or had walked out of Phil's life completely.

A seventh step is to follow the example of Jesus. He is the friend who sticks closer than a brother. Anyone can love when things are easy, but it takes fortitude to hang in with a person when the going gets tough. This is perseverance. In fact, Jesus stayed the closest when the difficulties were the worst. To follow love as a lifestyle means our perseverance will be severely tested. It is okay to take a vacation, but not to be a deserter. Try to keep the door open so that God can work through you. I have a number of people that I choose to call on a regular basis. I can't be everything they want or need, but if I stick close to them, I may meet some of their needs and even a few of their wants.

Loving is not like changing hats. Those who love do so with deliberate commitment. Loving is a part of who they are. It is a lifestyle which flows from the life of Christ within.

7

Does Love Have A Price Tag?

*N*ancy was known for her vibrant loving ways. She was a people person who always met people's needs or made them feel special. Her love life with God seemed to be intact with things going just great.

Then one day, almost without warning, she stopped. She withdrew from those she was loving and she withdrew from the people who loved her. Her husband and others were silent for a while, but eventually the questions had to be asked, "What has happened? What has gone wrong? Why have you changed so much?"

Nancy's answer was simple, straightforward and maybe a little cold. "I'm just not willing to pay the price anymore." When pressed for details she said, "I'm just not willing to be that open. I feel like I can't serve or be friendly anymore. I'm out of gas."

Jesus warned us that before we begin a project we need to count the cost. Notice his words. "Suppose one of you wants to build a tower. Will he not first sit down and estimate the cost to see if he has enough money to complete it? For if he lays the foundation and is not able to finish it, everyone who sees it will ridicule him, saying, 'This fellow began to build and was not able to finish' " (Lk 14:28-30).

Loving is not exactly like building a house, but it does demand careful evaluation. What will it cost you and me if we decide to adopt love as a life principle? It sounds great to be a loving person. Is it always that great? Are the benefits enough to sustain the effort? Why do we want to be loving in the first place?

The idea of loving is hard to grasp. On the one hand, we can read 1 Corinthians 13 and think, "It sounds so simple, I'll just do it." But on another occasion we may feel totally overwhelmed. I can't do what it takes to love. "Love is patient, love is kind. It does not envy, it does not boast, it is not proud. It is not rude, it is not self-seeking, it is not easily angered, it keeps no record of wrongs. Love does not delight in evil but rejoices with the truth. It always protects, always trusts, always hopes, always perseveres" (1 Cor 13:4-7). At best, loving as God intends it is a struggle. It just isn't natural. It cuts across our selfish natures.

The Struggles of Love

My good friend, DeLoss Friesen, has made some real sacrifices for me at times but rarely without a struggle. He became quite upset when I asked him to teach an extension class for me while I was getting ready to take part in filming a Christian movie. The cost was great. He would have to travel eighty miles each way.

"Why do you always get to do all the fun things?" he said in a raised voice. I waited silently knowing what would happen next. "I'm sorry," he said eventually. "I was just ticked."

I laughed and said, "That's okay. When you raised your voice I knew I had you."

I knew that choosing to do a loving thing for a person can be upsetting. When you count the cost and still decide to sacrifice, you don't always feel great about it. Dee still had to drive eighty miles, teach for three hours and then drive the eighty miles back home. He struggled to love me in this way, but he did it and he did it without bitterness. When I saw him the next day he shook my hand and said, "How did it go?" He didn't have to show concern about the filming. But he did.

Since then I have prayed, "God help me to be that kind of person when I struggle over what it costs to love my friends."

I have struggled too. One evening I came home at 6:30 tired and hungry. "Where is dinner?" I thought, "We always eat at 6:00 P.M. Where is Sandy?" I knew she gave lots of time to her friends and the younger women at church. She was to meet with Kristi that day, but they were supposed to be through by 6:00. About that time I heard laughter from the backyard and I realized they were enjoying fellowship together. I was embarrassed when I realized I was thinking, "They're not supposed to be having fun!" Fortunately I was able to regain control before I made a fool of myself.

I confessed my grumpiness to the Lord and said, "God I really do want to help Sandy in her important ministry even if I am acting like a fathead." After that my struggle subsided and I was able to actually enjoy the fact that I could do something which could support Sandy in her ministry of love. Luckily my mother had taught me a little bit about cooking.

Just as I have struggled to love Sandy enough to support her, she has also struggled to love me in the speaking, counseling and writing ministry that God has given me. It is difficult for her to spend evenings alone while I am speaking at a banquet or teaching a class. It is difficult for her not to get jealous when female clients of mine tell her that I am the only man that has ever understood them. Sometimes Sandy wants me to stay home with her, but I have to leave the house at 6:00 A.M. if I am going to get my writing done.

Just as our Lord gave of himself in order to love us, we must give of ourselves if we are to love each other. We only kid ourselves if we do not acknowledge that it is a struggle. I cannot read words like *patience, kindness,* or *being not envious, proud,* or *rude,* without realizing just how much I need God's love if I am to win the struggle to be a loving person.

John Powell therefore raises the very legitimate question, Is it worth it?

In fact, I would say that this is the major crisis facing contemporary society. *Is a life of love, which involves a permanent and unconditional commitment to the happiness of another, really the way to personal satisfaction and human fulfillment?* Or must one rather stay free and unencumbered from all such relationships in order to experience the pleasure, the power, and the variety of sensations which life can offer? Is personal satisfaction and gratification the most fulfilling life goal, or is the deepest meaning in life to be found only in a com-

mitted and permanent relationship of love? Should we
lay our lives and our persons on the line, or is it better
never to say "forever"?[1]

The Costs of Love

Love requires vulnerability. When we are willing to
reach out and love another, we are unmasked. Others
will see if we are really who we say we are. They will
know if we are sincere and consistent. Love cannot remain self-protective.

C. S. Lewis said it very powerfully:

I believe that the most lawless and inordinate loves are
less contrary to God's will than a self-invited and self-
protective lovelessness. It is like hiding the talent in a
napkin and for much the same reason "I knew thee
that thou were a hard man." Christ did not teach and
suffer that we might become, even in the natural
loves, more careful of our own happiness. If a man is
not uncalculating towards the earthly beloveds whom
he has seen, he is none the more likely to be so towards God whom he has not. We shall draw nearer
to God, not by trying to avoid the sufferings inherent
in all loves, but by accepting them and offering them
to Him; throwing away all defensive armour. If our
hearts need to be broken, and if He chooses this as the
way in which they should break, so be it.[2]

There are many people who have difficulty even in saying, "I love you." What if we say it and the other person
doesn't say it back? On the other hand, what if we reach
out in love and the other person misunderstands and
strikes back rather than appreciating our love?

When I was in high school, one of my friends tried to
express compassion to a great blue heron caught in an

animal trap. As Jim strained to release the trap the great bird escaped from under Jim's arm. In one strike of the bird's beak Jim lost an eye.

Many people said, "How dumb!" Why didn't he just kill the bird rather than taking the risk of trying to free it? The answer was clear, Jim loved animals. He became vulnerable to express this love. Not all of our vulnerability is this dangerous but it is clear that loving either man or beast will cost us something even if it is only time. So it is fair to ask, are we willing to be vulnerable enough in our loving to risk the same kind of response that Jesus received? Jesus was vulnerable, and he was rejected!

Another cost of loving is being willing to sacrifice. The most well-known Scripture of all says, "For God so loved . . . that he gave . . . " (Jn 3:16). Without loving there is no giving, and without giving there is no loving. Human love, like divine love, requires sacrifice. Notice carefully these words: "This is how we know what love is: Jesus Christ laid down his life for us. And we ought to lay down our lives for our brothers. If anyone has material possessions and sees his brother in need but has no pity on him, how can the love of God be in him? Dear children, let us not love with words or tongue but with actions and in truth" (1 Jn 3:16-18).

Giving doesn't happen automatically. It is a mindset. We have to be ready to give because the decisions to love are often instantaneous. We must ask ourselves, "Do I really want to see God bless others through me?"

One of the most difficult things for me to give is my time. I just don't like to give up my plans. I would like for God to send all the people I need to love to me at my convenience—preferably between ten in the morning and four in the afternoon. Why do people always need love from me when I have just settled down to watch a ball game or read a book? The answer is clear. To love is to be available.

The next time you cry out to God in the middle of the night, be sure to thank him for not taking his prayer phone off the hook. When you need him on a Saturday afternoon, be sure to thank him for being willing to take time out from the baseball game of the week!

After I have made the sacrifice, I usually feel satisfied and fulfilled. Before the decision I usually feel put out or angry. Down deep I do want to express the love God has put in me. But getting through the layers of selfishness is hard. Becoming the hands and feet of Jesus is a great privilege, but just because he wants to express his love through us doesn't mean that we will jump at every opportunity. Giving is always difficult. But on the other hand, "It is more blessed to give than to receive" (Acts 20:35).

A third cost of loving is being willing to be hurt. Maria sat in my office with tears streaming down her cheeks. She was hurt and she was angry. I knew Maria well enough to know how much she wanted to be a loving person. By being in my office she was telling me that she was paying the price. As I encouraged her to talk she began to vent some of her frustration.

Almost uncontrollably she blurted out, "People who need love are nasty. Sometimes they just get what they deserve." A friend had betrayed a deep trust. Now Maria was ready to blow.

After the emotional storm had subsided, I brought Maria back to the basic question, "What kind of a person do you want to be?"

She said, "I really do want to learn to love the way Jesus loves. I just don't want to get hurt in the process." Down deep Maria knew that you can't love without getting hurt, but at that moment she was grieving. "I'll be all right," she said. "I just need to give God a chance to recharge my batteries."

When we are hurt during our attempts to love, we need to guard against our major psychological enemy—bitterness. Being hurt isn't so tragic. Bruises will heal! Feelings will recover! Even relationships can be revitalized. The tragedy is when we continue to hurt ourselves by being bitter rather than forgiving. I encouraged Maria to acknowledge the hurt and then to ask God for the grace to go back to her friend with love rather than with bitterness. It cost her something, but she also gained something.

I remembered my labor of love as a child. My father had caught a wild horse for me. The poor pony was dirty, unfriendly and covered with lice and ticks. "He is going to take a lot of loving care," Dad said. I was game for the task and enthusiastically set out to love that horse to good health, good looks and good behavior. The only problem was he wouldn't let me close to him.

I chased him until I was almost exhausted. When I finally did corner him, he added insult by flinging his head and bumping me in the nose. I was bloodied and angry once again. More than once I thought, "No stupid horse is worth this. I've got plenty of other animals to love and they aren't so mean." This was all true, but down deep I realized that it was the horse that needed my special love and care. I knew what I had to do.

Increasing my dedication and dealing with my bitterness was necessary, but it didn't solve the problem. I still got stepped on. I still was slapped in the face by a tail filled with cockleburs. I was even thrown to the ground when I tried to sit on his back. Sometimes you have probably experienced the same discouragement when dealing with a cantankerous friend or family member. If you choose to become a loving person, you can get thrown unceremoniously on your behind. The problem comes when you interpret each hurt as an injury.

Our son Mike, the high-school wrestler, was hurt in a match. The trainer said, "The first thing we have to do, Mike, is see if you are hurt or injured. You can't wrestle without pain, but I will not let you go back and wrestle if you have an injury." His shoulder muscles had been painfully stretched but not torn. He was hurt but not injured. He gamely went back and finished the match.

There are times when we need spiritual trainers to help us evaluate our condition so we can decide how serious the problem is. If you are just hurt, going back to love the person who inflicted the pain may be the best thing you can do. On the other hand, if your interaction has stirred up deep pain which you are unable to handle, then you may be risking further injury. God did not intend for you to minister to everyone. There are some friendships that you may not be able to afford. You will not be effective as a Christlike lover of people if you are continually beaten. Prayer and the wise counsel of Christian friends will help you to know when you are just hurt and when you are injured.

Another important cost of loving is perseverance. As Sandy returned from a visit with a friend she was helping, she said, "This is going to be a long, long process. Anita needs so much to understand God's goodness and yet there are so many blocks."

As it turned out, Sandy's point was understated. Many months later she confessed to me, "It is a good thing that God didn't let me know how long this was going to take. I'm not sure I would have had faith enough to begin. I'm not sorry, but I have to admit that I am exhausted."

It helps to think about loving as a marathon rather than a hundred-yard dash. Jesus knew and knows about this kind of love. Notice John 13:1: "Having loved his own who were in the world, he now showed them the full extent of his love."

Christian growth usually involves behavior change, and behavior change always takes time. As you persevere with those God has called you to love, you may need to push them or pull them, exhort them or encourage them, even challenge them or chastize them. Regardless of what you are called on to do, you have to stick with them. As they see your faithfulness and your refusal to give up on them, they may refuse to give up on God or themselves.

Margaret said, "I don't think I really knew the meaning of love until I saw the way my friend stood with me time and time again. I realized that if God was anything like her, I wanted to know him better." Margaret's friend wasn't surprised because she knew that it was God's persevering love for her that had enabled her to hang in with Margaret. Perseverance costs, but it pays high love dividends too.

Finally, when we think of the costs of love, we need to include loneliness. You may not think of people who love as being lonely, but they are. As you reach out to others you may often wonder if anyone is concerned about you. Jim said, "I poured my life into that group of guys and at times I wasn't even sure that one of them cared about me. They took all that I could give, and at times when I needed help, it seemed like they were looking in another direction."

Jesus knew the cost of loving. At times he would sit down and weep. Just when he needed his disciples to understand, they got off on some tangent that pulled them into their own worlds and away from his. The takers were there when he offered what he had to give. Where were the comforters now that he himself was weary or overtaken with sorrow?

The ultimate in love and the ultimate in loneliness came together when Jesus died on the cross for us. "My God, my God, why have you forsaken me?" (Mk 15:34). The Lord's great triumph of love took him through the anguish of loneliness. If you too will be a lover of people you must be prepared to pay the price of loneliness.

Undoubtedly there are other costs of loving which you will encounter. The good things in life are not free, and the great things in life usually are costly. But it is worth it. Just as Jesus' love transformed you and me, God will use your love to change others.

8

WHY DOES GOD LOVE US ANYWAY?

Y*ou don't love me," Julie said to her older brother.*

"Yes, I do," Billy replied.

"No, you don't," Julie persisted. "You only say you do because I'm your little sister."

"I love you," Billy said, "*even* if you are my little sister."

Julie wouldn't give up. "I'll bet you just say you love me because Mom and Dad said you should. You probably don't really love me."

Billy, looking annoyed, walked away as though he was trying to win the argument with silence.

It worked for awhile and then Julie took her final shot, "I'll bet you just love me because my birthday is tomor-

row and you want me to give you some of my birthday
cake."

It was amusing to watch Billy and Julie argue over the
why of love, but it isn't as much fun to struggle personally with why God loves us. Why does God love us any-
way? Just what is his motivation? Could it be pity?
How about pride? Is it because he needs us? None of
these questions seem to lead us to an understanding of
his great love. Let's consider a few other possibilities.

Loving Zeros?

First, does God love us because we are zeros? I don't
believe so. He wants us to be servants but he never asks
us to be zeros or worms. Such people, in fact, usually
make bad servants because they do not have the
strength to give to others when they are struggling to
survive emotionally themselves.

I believe God loves us because of what we are, not
because of what we aren't. So what are we? First, we are
his creation. That in itself makes us special. He created
us and he loved us. Even when we refused to love back
he still loved us. "God demonstrates his own love for us
in this: While we were still sinners, Christ died for us"
(Rom 5:8).

God's love for us flows out of the fact that we are his
creation and that he has chosen to pour out his love on
his creation—not because we earn it by being either
more (sinless) or less (zeros).

There is another reason we are special. God loves all
of his creation, but he gave human beings the unique
ability to love back. This reciprocity of love puts us on
a level with God that animals, plants or even whole solar
systems do not share. Idols can't love, but even pieces of

stone or wood can control their subjects by fear. God, on the other hand, doesn't want us to return his love out of fear but out of confidence and assurance. "There is no fear in love. But perfect love drives out fear, because fear has to do with punishment" (1 Jn 4:18). We are loved because God saw that what he made was good and desired to have fellowship with us.

God doesn't control us with fear or with his power. I once heard my son Mark yell, "I hope that makes you feel like a big man. Because you're stronger, you try to make us do what you want." Mark wasn't impressed with his larger comrade's attempt at a power play. Interestingly enough, God chose not to "make us" return his love. He does not play the big man. His love is patient and genuine. When we think of his great power and his patience, it is easy to make the mistake of feeling that he may love us out of pity, somewhat like an elephant loving a flea. The Bible says it is more like that of a father and his children. "As a father has compassion on his children so the LORD has compassion on those who fear him . . . But from everlasting to everlasting the LORD's love is with those who fear him" (Ps 103:13, 17).

Somehow a great and untouchable God, a truly big man is able to love us on an equal basis. I do not mean he stoops to our level. What I mean is that he is a person and loves us on a person-to-person basis. Jesus Christ, the God-man, brought God's love to us on a down-to-earth, understandable level. "Therefore, since we have a great high priest who has gone through the heavens, Jesus the Son of God, let us hold firmly to the faith we profess. For we do not have a high priest who is unable to sympathize with our weaknesses, but we have one who has been tempted in every way, just as we are—yet

was without sin. Let us then approach the throne of
grace with confidence, so that we may receive mercy and
find grace to help us in our time of need" (Heb 4:14-16).

Our concept of love is so dominated by romantic no-
tions, we need to ask if this is the way God loves us.
Does he find us so exciting that he can't resist? The
notion is a bit ridiculous. Historically our exciting nature
has been drowned in the sea of sin and self-deception.
God fishes us out and dries us off only to have us dive
back in again. Hardly the stuff that romance is made of.

Some romantics are sustained by a belief that the one
they love will change. Is God this kind of "hopeless romantic"? Not at all. He knows what we are like better
than we do ourselves. History tells the tale of women
and men running from, not to, God's love. We seem to
have changed all right, but rarely for the better. God
takes pleasure in our love, but is the ultimate realist. He
knows we will fail him, but he still chooses to love us.
That's the kind of love I need.

God Desires Our Fellowship

When all is said and done, one answer seems to stand
out. God desires our fellowship.

A superintelligent being, God, created people with in-
telligence so that he could love and interact with them.
The Fiddler on the Roof has helped many people to grasp this
concept because of the way Tevye engages in frequent
conversation with God. The playwrights did a marvelous
job of conveying the idea that both Tevye and God were
excited about the dialog.

The book of Genesis points to the fellowship between
God and his people. He walked and talked with Adam
and Eve. He was very close with Enoch. He spent time

with Noah. And God poured out his blessing on Abraham. None of this was necessary. He didn't need their fellowship. God did it because he wanted to do so.

We can better understand God's desire for fellowship by looking at the way Jesus related to people. Jesus, God in the flesh, seemed to always have time to talk. He was a very social being. Even when he was facing his death, he wanted people close by. His arms always seemed to be outstretched. His lips seemed to always whisper the same phrase, "Come to me." Since we see the Father in Jesus (Jn 14:7), we know this is God's attitude toward us.

Regardless of what God gets out of loving us, the exciting fact is that you and I get a tremendous amount out of being loved. Just as I benefited from the wonderful love my parents had for me, so I benefit from the love my heavenly Father has for me. My parents loved me for my own sake and so does God.

To say that God loves us for our own sake has two important messages. First, he loves us for who we are. And second, he loves us so we can be all he wants us to be. These two thoughts are put together neatly in a saying I heard recently: "God loves us just the way we are but he loves us too much to let us stay that way."

How Can I Experience This Love?

Even if we could fully answer the question, "Why does God love us?" we might still fall short of experiencing what it means to be so loved. One of my friends said, "I have known God, or at least known about God intellectually, for a long time. In the last few years I have made it my goal to let that love touch my emotions. I want to 'be in love' with God in a new way."

I too have been on a similar quest. My wife has been